The Tai Chi
Two-Person Dance

The Tai Chi Two-Person Dance

Tai Chi with a Partner

Jonathan Russell

With photographs of T.T. Liang

North Atlantic Books
Berkeley, California

Published by
North Atlantic Books
P.O. Box 12327
Berkeley, California 94712

Cover and book design by Jonathan Russell and Paula Morrison
Photographs and illustrations by Jonathan Russell

Printed in Canada

The Tai Chi Two-Person Dance: Tai Chi with a Partner is sponsored by the Society for the Study of Native Arts and Sciences, a nonprofit educational corporation whose goals are to develop an educational and crosscultural perspective linking various scientific, social, and artistic fields; to nurture a holistic view of arts, sciences, humanities, and healing; and to publish and distribute literature on the relationship of mind, body, and nature.

North Atlantic Books' publications are available through most bookstores. For further information, call 800-337-2665 or visit our website at www.northatlanticbooks.com.

Substantial discounts on bulk quantities are available to corporations, professional associations, and other organizations. For details and discount information, contact our special sales department.

Library of Congress Cataloging-in-Publication Data

Russell, Jonathan, 1952–
    The tai chi two-person dance : tai chi with a partner / by Jonathan
Russell.
        p. cm.
    ISBN 1-55643-441-3 (pbk.)
    1. Tai chi. 2. Dance. I. Title.
    GV504.R87 2003
    613.7'148—dc22

                                    2003018383

1 2 3 4 5 6 7 8 9 TRANS 09 08 07 06 05 04

Boston 1985

This book is dedicated to the memory of Master T.T. Liang.

Tai Chi was his passion and the Tai Chi Two-Person Dance his dream.
I first started work on this project twenty-five years ago. For years I would meet Sunday mornings with T. T. Liang to take photographs of individual postures and discuss with him the nuances of how to accurately portray and explain them. After far too many delays, it was with great pleasure that I was finally able to show him the finished manuscript. He died two weeks later.

This book is a part of his legacy. It is intended for his many students as well as all other Tai Chi enthusiasts.

Acknowledgments

First and foremost I wish to acknowledge my debt of gratitude to T.T. Liang for his patience and understanding over our many years together. What he gave me can't be given, and for this I will always be grateful.

I would also like to express thanks to the following:

To my wife Saori, whose support and encouragement got this "dance" out of my head and onto the printed page. She created the "time-line" format for the pictures and had the unenviable task of reading my first drafts. This book truly would never have been written without her.

I want to thank my old friend and fellow student, Stuart Olson, for his generosity in making available to me his considerable research and writings on the history of Tai Chi.

To Susan Spero, for coming to the studio all those Sunday mornings to model for the photographs with Liang.

To my student Le Nguyen, for posing for the photographs of every beat of every posture of the dance.

To my students Jael Weisman and Sally Goodman, for their inestimable help and perseverance in correcting the manuscript.

To my student Charla, for kindly taking over my classes when I needed time to write.

To John Makropolis and Allan Shapiro, for their input and, more importantly, for their kind understanding of what it means to be fellow students of T. T. Liang.

And lastly, to my friend Sally, who demonstrated that it's possible to get something done—even when there's no time to do it.

Table of Contents

Foreword

by Stuart Olson

Finding a new depth and dimension to the art of Tai Chi within the bulk of available literature is rare. This book uniquely provides a long-over-due record of an important facet of Tai Chi practice—*the two-person training exercises.* The majority of present-day practitioners of Tai Chi know only of the solo form, primarily an exercise in developing balance, relaxation, and *qi.* Just practicing the solo form, however, cannot bring you to the higher levels of the art. Acquiring what are known as the intrinsic energy skills (*jin*) is the very goal and purpose of the two-person training exercises.

The Tai Chi Two-Person Dance presented here is the unique integration of the three traditional training practices: *T'ui Shou* (Sensing-Hands), *Ta Lu Shou* (Greater Rolling-Back Hands), and *San Shou* (Dispersing-Hands). Traditionally, these three training methods were practiced separately, but herein they are combined in one complete set. Master T.T. Liang arranged his Tai Chi Two-Person Dance, consisting of 178 Postures, more than thirty years ago. Having studied with fifteen accomplished masters in Taiwan, he combined all his knowledge and skills into arranging this one set of complete exercises so that it would be easier for his students to learn. His invention of the Tai Chi Two-Person Dance as well as his adapting music to both it and the Tai Chi solo form are his contribution to the art of Tai Chi.

No other student of Master Liang learned or understood the actual function of the Tai Chi Two-Person Dance better than Jonathan Russell, his most senior student. So it is with genuine sincerity that I find myself very enthusiastic about the publication of this book, and I highly recommend it to all Tai Chi students. Presently, Tai Chi is being more or less promoted as a health exercise, which is just one aspect of the art. So it gladdens me to see the advanced aspects being presented here, and

Jonathan has done a superb job in writing and organizing the material.

Even though it can be said that the Two-Person Dance focuses on the self-defense side of Tai Chi, this "self-defense" can be looked at from a different perspective. To me, the meaning is actually closer to "defense against the self" than that of "defending the self." For it is "I" who makes the mistakes allowing my defeat or injury when being attacked. "I" can only be harmed or defeated through my own mistakes in dealing with an opponent.

Many students over the years have told us that they are not interested in learning how to fight. The Tai Chi Two-Person Dance, however, is not actual fighting—it is disciplining yourself to react in the most natural and relaxed manner possible when confronted with aggression, conflict, or in any situation.

Skills gained from the Two-Person Dance, such as *interpreting* and *neutralizing,* are meant to be used controlling your own self and the opponent rather than aggressively fighting. Tai Chi bases itself upon developing heightened sensitivity, increased perceptivity, and application of relaxation and softness against tension and hardness. To truly master Tai Chi, the exercises in the Tai Chi Two-Person Dance must be practiced. Otherwise, as Master Liang frequently told his students, "You will only know half the art and be handicapped both in developing qi and defending yourself in a time of emergency."

The Tai Chi Two-Person Dance is the apex of the art of Tai Chi. No serious student of Tai Chi should overlook it. But like many of the deeper aspects of Tai Chi, it has either not been presented or was presented poorly to Western culture. This book, however, is unequalled by anything previously published. Indeed, having read everything available in both English and Chinese on this subject, I can say without hesitation that this is the best presentation yet compiled. I applaud Jonathan Russell's efforts here, knowing first-hand how long and hard he worked to bring all the necessary pieces together to complete this project. It is his "masterpiece" and a very valuable addition to the "good books" of Tai Chi literature.

—Stuart Alve Olson

Author of *Steal My Art: The Life and Times of T'ai Chi Master T.T. Liang*

Introduction

My best friend while I was in my teens was a seventy-plus-year-old former high-ranking customs official from China, T.T Liang.

The difference in our ages and experiences was remarkable. The intersection of me, with no life experiences to speak of, and him, with far too many, often led to humorous situations. Once, after a youthful misadventure, I landed in jail for a few hours and came back to complain to him about this obvious "injustice." His laughing response was, "At least it was free rent with meals included!" He went on to relate how he had been captured by the Japanese in 1940 and imprisoned. His subordinates were brought before him and tortured, and his feet were beaten with bats. There was not much that this eighteen-year-old with only a crushed ego could say in response to that. . . .

Liang had gone from being a top customs officer under Chiang Kai Shek in China to facing a deathly illness in Taiwan. Given six months to live, he

T.T. Liang and the author in 1973

pursued Tai Chi and slowly regained his health. Twenty-plus years later in 1963, he was invited by the famous Tai Chi teacher, Cheng Man Ching, to accompany him to New York City to translate and teach at the United Nations. From there Liang went to Boston, where I found him in 1969 teaching classes out of his one-room apartment with the Murphy bed up.

Somewhere in the midst of grocery shopping, translating old Chinese texts and just "hanging out," he taught me the art of Tai Chi—an art based on his experience, innovation, and curiosity.

Constantly learning and questioning, Liang once packed up and went back to Taiwan—leaving me to run the studio. He had heard of a teacher that knew the practical use, or martial arts use, of the long tassel that hangs from the handle of the double-edged Tai Chi sword. It turned out that this teacher was a practitioner of Shaolin, a "hard style" martial art. Liang studied with him and then translated what he learned of the tassel into the soft movements of the Tai Chi sword forms—thus recovering a technique that had been all but lost. (This relentless questioning and learning also had a humorous side. I had to survive many semesters of his going back to Harvard evening school at the age of eighty to learn about 18th-century English literature.)

My reason for giving this history is that it forms the background for this book. The Two-Person Dance is one of T.T. Liang's major contributions to the art of Tai Chi. It was born out of his relentless pursuit of the fundamental principles behind this exercise and the search for ways to teach them. While living in Taiwan, he had sought out teachers who knew different advanced forms of Tai Chi, the two-person forms performed with a partner. Liang, breaking away from the cultural norm of studying with just one "Master," learned from each teacher his particular two-person set. Later, as though with pieces of a puzzle, he put together all of the different San Shou, Ta Lu, and Pushing Hands forms he had learned in one continuous string of 175 postures. To keep students from competing and using force while performing this exercise together, he drew on his experiences in the dance halls of Shanghai while an officer working with the British. He developed a dance-like approach by adding music and timing with beats. This kept the practitioner's focus not on the idea or intent of fighting but on further developing the skills of Tai Chi.

When Liang and I set up our first studio together in Boston in the early '70s he was insistent upon describing what we were teaching as a "dance." At the time, I didn't like this idea. In my mind the last thing in the world I wanted to be associated with was the word "dance." I was learning and teaching a martial art! During all those years that he and I had studios together in Boston, most students never realized that they were coming to a studio called "The Tai Chi Dance Association." Even while I was writing this book friends advised me not to include "dance" in the title, as it would alienate Tai Chi practitioners and especially martial arts enthusiasts. Over the years, though, I have come to realize that Liang was right: the concept of dance is important, even integral, to an understanding of Tai Chi Chuan. It is truly a dance of opposites.

Poster for studio in Boston, 1973

Thirty years have passed since Liang and I co-founded The Tai Chi Dance Association in Boston. I have gone on to teach Tai Chi from coast to coast and watched as Tai Chi became part of the American cultural landscape. This is in no small part due to the efforts of T.T. Liang. His book *T'ai Chi for Health and Self-Defense* (Vintage Press) has become one of the most popular books in the English language on the subject. This once-obscure exercise has now come into the public consciousness. The stereotypical image of an old Asian man practicing the slow movements of the Tai Chi exercise is no longer the extent of Tai Chi in the U.S. On the contrary, the average student in my classes is a 26- to 35-year-old woman. As an example of how diverse and widespread Tai Chi has become in our community, my clients in just the past few years have included such disparate groups as MAC Cosmetics, Virgin Atlantic, 24-Hour Fitness, Bank of America, and even a French Peugeot car dealers' association.

This book is for the large, diverse, and ever-growing community of Tai Chi enthusiasts. It doesn't matter which of the many different styles of Tai Chi one is familiar with; the movements described in this book are common to all. Precisely detailed posture descriptions and clear photographs will guide students through the sequence of movements. While working with a partner, a student will come to understand the meanings and uses of the postures he or she has been practicing individually. This dance will take them to the next step in the learning of Tai Chi—

harmonizing one's movements with a partner and developing sensitivity of feeling through the body. The skills of interpreting movements and of adhering without resistance or letting go of your partner can now be worked on, developed, and refined.

T.T. Liang and the author, demonstrating Tai Chi Dance at William CC Chen Studio, New York City, 1989.

1

What Is the Tai Chi Two-Person Dance?

When asked what the name of the symbol in Figure 1 is, most people will answer "the yin/yang symbol." This is a good answer because it describes the image accurately. The white represents *Yang* (solid, hard, male, etc.) and the black represents *Yin* (empty, soft, female, etc.) hence it's common name: the *Yin/Yang symbol.* But the actual name is the "Tai Chi Tu" (Grand Ultimus or Grand Terminus). It portrays an underlying principle of Chinese thought—that the essence or energy behind all things, from rocks to animals (inanimate to animate), alternately takes the form of yin and of yang. When yang reaches its extreme, it gives way to yin; when yin reaches its extreme, it gives way to yang. The harmony produced by the continuous transformation of opposites, of one into the other, is basic to Far Eastern culture and is the foundation for the ideas that make up the martial art of its namesake: Tai Chi Chuan (*Chuan* meaning *"fist"* or *"martial aspect"*).

Figure 1

Legend has it that the founder of Tai Chi, Chang San Feng, woke up one morning to find a bird and a snake fighting each other outside his bedroom window. He watched in awe as neither of them could take advantage of the other. Each time the snake struck out at the crane it would deftly step aside and sweep the snake away with its outstretched wing. Each time the crane would strike with its pointed beak toward the snake, the snake would recoil and counter-attack as if in one motion. The grace and subtlety of this intertwining dance impressed him greatly. Each animal's movements mirrored the other's. When one struck out, the other immediately neutralized the incoming blow with one part of its body while simultaneously attacking with another part. This dance was to Chang San Feng a perfect expression of the interaction of "Yin and Yang" symbolized in the Tai Chi Tu. From this he developed a martial art of round and circular movements that emphasized an awareness of the hard and the soft attributes according to the variations of yin and yang.

Tai Chi puts emphasis on the subtle skills of sensitivity and listening to the body to attain high levels of ability while other styles of martial arts emphasize speed overcoming slowness, strength overcoming weakness, and aggression over calmness. Tai Chi training highlights tranquility within motion and motion within tranquility. One confronts the forceful and unyielding with the gentle and yielding.

The student is asked to relax and observe his or her balance. To do this one first learns a dance-like solo form, which can vary from 36 to 150 postures. Each posture consists of a martial movement involving an imaginary partner (hence the name "shadow boxing"). These movements are practiced slowly, with emphasis on developing a focused internal awareness of one's own balance, position, and state of relaxation.

When one has developed a firm footing (central equilibrium), the next step is to learn to move and interact with a partner. One can now put into context the slow and graceful movements that he or she has been practicing alone. Learning the solo form is learning the basic vocabulary of the language of Tai Chi. Putting that vocabulary into a conversation is the two-person dance. The participants enter into a dialogue with each other. One movement will initiate and set into motion the next, so that a language of mutual body awareness is developed. The student must not only observe himself or herself, but now must interpret and "answer" the movements of a partner as well. This physical interplay of opposites is what characterizes the Tai Chi Dance.

The two-person forms combine the previously mentioned internal observation with an external awareness of a real partner's movements and balance. Through softness and yielding the skills of listening, interpreting, and adhering (without resistance or letting go of) your partner are now worked on and developed. Different kinds of exercises within the two person dance refine the student's ability to interact with incoming stimuli and to harmonize with a partner's ever-changing manifestations of yin into yang and vice versa. The dance partners are now ready to emulate the legendary crane and snake.

Chang San Feng, founder of Tai Chi Chuan, at Wu Tang mountain, watching the bird and snake matching wits. Painted by T.T. Liang

Yang Cheng Fu demonstrating "kick with sole."

2

A Little History

The history of Tai Chi Chuan has been written about extensively and encompasses many different theories of how it was handed down. It appears, though, to have been around for thousands of years and is an expression of Chinese Taoist thought and philosophy. It was first recorded as being taught within the Chen family of Honan Province more than three hundred years ago. As was common with most specialized training during that time, Tai Chi was taught in private, and outsiders were not allowed access.

Legend has it that Yang Lu Chan in the early 19th century posed as a servant for the Chen family in order to secretly observe and learn Tai Chi. Yang was eventually discovered, but his abilities and temperament were such that he was allowed to stay and learn. After a number of years the head of the family, Chen Chang Hsing, called together all of his students. He said that he had wanted to hand down his art to his family but they were unable to learn it. Instead, he told them, an outsider named Yang Lu Chan had managed to learn his entire art and was now ready to leave.

From the Chen family village, Yang Lu Chan went to Beijing, where he was hired by the Royal Family. Through time his skill and the art of Tai Chi became well known. His grandson, Yang Cheng Fu, is credited with popularizing the Yang Style of Tai Chi as it is known today.

The origins of the Tai Chi two-person exercises are difficult to trace. The classical writings about Tai Chi contain many references to applications and skills, but not to the actual two-person training exercises. Although records indicate that two-person training methods existed as far back as 1200 C.E., they never really became public until the mid-1900s, when the first detailed explanation of them came from a student of the Yang family, Chen Kung (or Yearning K. Chen). His book is reportedly based on the records and notes of the original Yang family training manuals. He describes three different categories of two-person exercises. They are: *Pushing Hands (T'ui Shou), Greater Rolling-Back Hands (Ta Lu Shou),* and *Dispersing-Hands (San Shou).* Practiced individually, these were all originally employed to develop different skills.

Pushing Hands (T'ui Shou)

Pushing Hands (or "out-reaching, sensing hand") is primarily an exercise to develop the skills of *Warding-Off, Rolling-Back, Pressing,* and *Pushing.* These four skills were considered a necessary foundation for learning to work with a partner, so Pushing Hands was the first two-person technique taught to students. It is taught first with the feet in a fixed position and later with active stepping back and forth along a straight line.

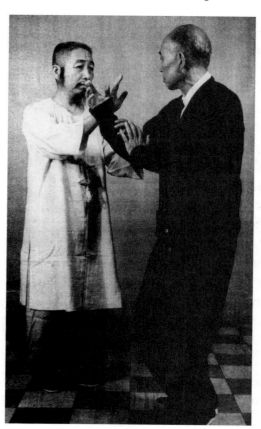

Cheng Man Ching and T.T. Liang demonstrating "Pushing Hands"

One partner (A) will *Push* his partner's forearm with both hands while that partner (B) *Wards-Off* the push by shifting his weight back and then turning the incoming push to the side in what's called a *Rolling Back* motion. Partner A will then *Press* to the partner's chest with the back of his wrist and forearm. Partner B will let this press pass by them while attaching their hands to A's forearm. B is now in a position to push A and repeat the above movements. The hand movements of both partners at first move along a horizontal plane and gradually advance to being more three-dimensional or circular. The interchange of these four movements constitutes the exercise of Pushing Hands.

Within this exercise the students start to observe and detect their own and their partners' ever-changing use of force and fluctuating center of gravity. To do this, the partners maintain with their hands an unbroken light contact with each other. They try not to resist each other as well as to not let go. Each partner focuses on detecting the other one's slightest movement. Repeating these four postures over and over, the students refine their sense of touch so that eventually they can naturally perceive their partners' every action.

Greater Rolling-Back Hands (Ta Lu Shou)

Greater Rolling-Back Hands (Ta Lu Shou) focuses on the Pulling, Splitting, Elbowing, and Shouldering techniques of Tai Chi. These four advancing movements are each countered by a retreating rolling-back movement. Hence the name: Greater Roll Back. Each of the four movements is performed with an accompanying step. Pull is an attempt to grasp the hand or wrist in a downward movement. Split is an attempt to lock the wrist and elbow of one arm. Elbow strike aims for the heart, which segues into a strike from the Shoulder. One partner steps forward in one direction, executing the above movements, while the other retreats backward while performing defensive movements (Roll Back) to neutralize the incoming strikes.

Practiced repeatedly these combined movements are sometimes referred to as "The Four Corners Operations," since they are performed toward the four diagonal directions or corners. This exercise focuses on stepping and positioning in relationship to your partner and helps to coordinate the movements of the hands and feet with the rest of the body.

T.T. Liang performing "Split" from the Ta Lu exercise in Taiwan with "the school teacher" Liu Chiun-fu.

Dispersing-Hands (San Shou)

Dispersing-Hands (San Shou) was most likely developed by Yang Lu Chan. The most complex of the three categories, the original Dispersing-Hands exercise consisted of 88 postures. This exercise makes use of the practical applications of the individual Tai Chi postures within the solo form and their corresponding countering methods.

Unlike Pushing Hands, with its in-line or fixed steps, and Greater Roll Back, with its straight line movements, Dispersing Hands demands circling dynamic footwork from the two partners. This set aims to develop a natural sense of maintaining correct distance and positioning with one's partner while executing the skills of: "neutralize," "adhere," and "issue." Using a choreographed series of postures, the partners will repeatedly interact back and forth using these three techniques.

When one partner is being pushed by the other, he will *neutralize* the effect of the incoming force by diverting it or moving with it (not resisting) until its power has dissipated. Next, by *adhering* to a partner one will maneuver him into an off-balance or "defective" position. At this point one will *issue* force to the partner. An important point is that when issuing force (energy), the student is not just blindly pushing. Instead, he or she is carefully detecting the partner's center of gravity and "line of balance" and then issuing an elastic or tenacious force focused across that line.

The ability to fully integrate all of the above categories is the goal of the Tai Chi two-person exercises. It prepares the student for practicing "free form" with a partner without any prearranged choreography. In this unfixed method any one of the movements of Pushing Hands, Greater Roll Back and Dispersing Hands can be adopted freely and neutralized whenever confronted. Both partners can distinguish clearly between the insubstantial and substantial (yin and yang) movements of their partner so that the dialogue of "neutralize," "adhere," and "issue" takes place naturally. This is the apex of the art of Tai Chi.

T.T. Liang's contribution to this history is his combining of all these traditionally separate two-person training methods into one single exercise that he calls The Tai Chi Two-Person Dance. He learned the original 88-posture Yang style San Shou set from Hsiung Yang-Hou (who studied with Yang Shao Hou) in Taiwan. To this Liang added the Pushing Hands exercises and also included the Greater Roll Back exercises taught to him by Wang Yen-nien (who studied with Chang Ch'in Lin) and Cheng Man-ch'ing (who studied with Yang Cheng Fu).

He also added another important dimension in the study of two-person exercises with his inclusion of tempo and beats. While studying and teaching the San Shou exercises he noticed that his students could not resist using force with each other. Their practice would escalate more often into a competitive brawl than an exercise of sensitivity. To correct this tendency he drew on his experiences in the dance halls of Shanghai. He developed a dance-like approach to Tai Chi by adding music and timing with beats. This created a structure within which the partners could focus on the intricacies of their movements without regard to winning or losing.

T.T. Liang performing San Shou with Inoch Yu, Taiwan 1955.

T.T. Liang "demonstrating his form" in a dance hall in Shanghai, 1942.

3

Tai Chi with Music

While performing the postures of the two-person dance there is a tendency toward competition. Each posture has a practical use, and it is tempting to implement it "to score a point." Students will naturally begin to focus on winning and losing and start to struggle. Aggressive actions enter into the movements and interfere with the ability to listen to and interpret the movements of one's partner. Competitively testing and comparing of abilities at this stage interferes with learning and promotes tension and anxiety. Rather than paying attention to uprooting your opponent, you need instead to pay attention to your own root and closely observe your partner.

Performing the dance with music allows both partners to focus on the flow and rhythm of each posture. Both partners know exactly when the movement is going to be executed, so any thought of competition is eliminated. When there is no concern for protecting oneself, one can focus instead on qualities of movement, body position, and balance. Knowing the sequence and timing of the postures also limits the possibilities of unknown movements and for beginners any worry associated with unpredictability. Developing skills with a calm attitude, through repetition, ensures that the student will not develop bad habits.

The correct flow of the movements is sustained within the beats. At first students might feel that they are moving in almost a mechanical fashion from one beat to another. The movements might seem angular or "box-like." As one becomes familiar, though, with connecting a movement to a beat, one begins to conceal or "round the corners" of the posture. There now develops a flowing interaction between the two dance partners that maintains the subtleties and nuance of intent of each posture.

The beats also clearly define which partner is taking the initiative. Unlike traditional Western dance, where the male partner leads and initiates movements while the female follows, the "lead" in Tai Chi switches from partner to partner with every posture. When your partner takes the lead you follow and then neutralize his incoming action. Your neutralizing will set up your next move, in which you then take the initiative. The beats define this interaction so that neither partner rushes the movement.

Contained within the beats is the technique of *neutralize, adhere,* and *issue.* Every posture maintains these three important maneuvers within the count of four beats. On the first and second beat you move yourself into a superior position with your partner *(adhere).* On the third beat you relax, remain still and gather intention. On the last beat you execute the posture *(issue).* On that last beat, as well, your partner will get out of the way of *(neutralize)* your incoming movement and proceed, as above, to *adhere* and *issue.* This interchange is repeated over and over again throughout the Two-Person Dance.

Most importantly, the music creates an attitude between the partners that is one of enjoyment, fun, and relaxation. In the words of T.T. Liang:

> *I introduced rhythm so that the postures can be practiced to music slowly, effortlessly, and evenly, to create coordination of body and mind. I use the term "dance" so the student will automatically associate it with relaxation and having fun. If I called it Tai Chi Boxing, then everyone will become aggressive and want to fight.*

4

Practice Points

The primary focus while performing the Tai Chi Dance with a partner is on learning to feel and interpret your partner's movements, to be able to detect their center of balance and position in relationship to yours. By staying relaxed and moving smoothly without hard angles, without hesitating, and without creating obstructions, the student will try to identify—in themselves and in their partner—what are called "defect positions." These are the places where one is off balance, too hard, too soft, or over-extended, to name just a few. To accomplish this there are many things that the Tai Chi practitioner needs to keep in mind. The following is a list of useful points to consider while engaging a partner.

Relaxing: Freedom of movement is achieved by not holding tension in the body. One refrains from tensing the muscles or using force against a partner.

Visual Focus: Quieting the mind, one's attention should be concentrated. Your eyes remain looking forward or on your partner's chest (sternum). You don't focus on any one aspect or movement of your partner. Peripheral vision is used instead.

Touch: Each partner remains, at all times, in light contact with the other, never resisting and never letting go. Do not use too much force. Your partner will feel this and try to counter it. One hand, at least, must stay attached to your partner; otherwise the ability to feel their movements is severed, thus making it difficult to locate their center of gravity.

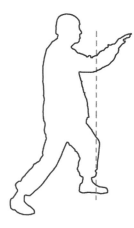

Leaning: The body remains upright without leaning forward or backward. In a forward push do not allow your knee to go beyond your toes or your elbow to pass beyond your knee.

Arm Position: Your shoulders are relaxed and your elbows are bent and relaxed downward. Try not to raise them up.

Positioning: Special attention is paid to positioning with your partner. Dance partners sometimes refer to the space between them as a dynamic "active space." You don't want to get too close to your partner or too far away. Too close and your balance is exposed; you may become off-balance. Too far away and there is no ability to "read" and "listen" to your partner's movements.

Shadowing: You try to not allow any separation between you and your partner. In this respect you become like their shadow. Wherever and whenever they move, you move. When they retreat you follow, when they advance you retreat. You never allow any separation or "gaps." This means no sudden letting go, no slowing down, and no inappropriately angular movements.

Attaching: Never forcefully grab your partner. When meeting your partner's incoming movements, you don't want to clash with them but instead you match their speed in order to lightly attach, engage, and blend with them in a circular motion. A good example of this is two spinning tops.

If they are spinning at the same speed in opposite directions and the two touch each other, each will have little effect on the other's balance. The point of contact is moving in the same direction so each side matches and blends with the other.

Stepping: When stepping forward or backward—or in any direction— you do not throw your weight onto the stepping foot but instead you consciously place your foot down and then shift your weight into it. This is one aspect of what in Tai Chi is called "carefully distinguishing the substantial from the insubstantial."

Central Equilibrium: One is ever-watchful for one's own and the partner's central pivot point or center of gravity. Is the center of gravity too high or is it over-extended beyond its base? While in motion, central equilibrium can be likened to a spinning top whose central pivot point is maintained and remains upright. When still it can be likened to a cone with its widest part on the floor.

Double-Weighting: Double-weighting is an undesirable state of being off balance while in motion. It is when you divide your weight equally between both feet. This exposes your center of gravity and hinders your ability to adjust your position in relation to your partner. In motion you should remain "single-weighted," where you transition your weight carefully from one foot to the other in order to correctly initiate, without being off balance, a movement toward your partner.

The defect of double-weighting can also be detected in pushing. A correct push is executed using the opposite hand from the foot that initiates it. In other words, if your weight is on your left foot you will want to push with your right hand. You also never want to push with both hands at the same time. One hand will push while the other remains attached to your partner in a back-up role.

Mirroring Your Partner: At all times try to remain facing your partner. Like a boat with a heavy keel always righting itself in the water, you want to always come back to facing your partner in every move.

Moving as One Unit: The body moves as one—not as separate pieces. No one part of the body acts alone but instead moves in harmony with the entire body. The most common fault is found with hand movements. There is a Tai Chi saying to describe this defect: "You have hands all over your body but Tai Chi has nothing to do with hands." When the hands move, they do not move independently, but instead the impetus for their actions comes from the feet and the legs and is then directed by the torso out to the hands. The movement of a horizontal bicycle wheel accurately describes this. Imagine your hands are the perimeter of the wheel, your arms are the spokes and your waist (torso) is the hub. If the hub (your waist) turns an inch, then the outside perimeter of the wheel (your hands) will turn a foot. Your hands have moved, *but not independently.* They move because the hub (your torso) has turned.

This relationship of the torso commanding the body is described metaphorically by the Chinese general of ancient times commanding his troops in war. The general (your mind) oversees the battlefield and gives the commands to his troops via his flag bearer. The flag bearer (your waist and torso) puts up the correct flags, giving instructions to the troops (your body and limbs). The troops move only in accordance with the instructions that are indicated by the flags.

Folding: This is a technique where you fill any space or gap between you and your partner. When you detect resistance on one part of your body, you allow yourself to "fold" another part of your body into that gap to strike your partner. For example, if she grabs your wrist you will strike her with your elbow. If she blocks your elbow you will then strike her with your shoulder. If she blocks your shoulder you will then strike with your forehead.

5

Sung

Before we can look at the advanced skills of Tai Chi we first have to understand the Chinese word *sung*. It is roughly translated into English as "relax." The idea of *sung*, though, is much more complex than merely to relax. It does not mean to collapse but instead embodies the idea of letting go of your muscular tensions while at the same time retaining an active and alert attention. The result of this kind of relaxing is a lowering of your center of gravity and the gaining of what the Chinese descriptively call a "root." This is where, like a tree, your feet are firmly rooted to the floor. A good analogy is the comparison of a solid steel pipe with the equivalent weight of steel made into a linked chain. The pipe, lying on the ground, is relatively easy to pick up, since one can locate the center of the pipe (its center of gravity) and lift. The chain, on the other hand, is not so easy to lift off the ground. Because it is not rigid it is difficult to find any center of gravity. Every single link has to be gathered before it can be lifted off the ground. In this sense it becomes heavier and more attached ("rooted") to the ground than the rigid pipe. One's body, similar to the chain, relaxes with no tension held in any of the limbs and joints.

All of the underlying principles of Tai Chi and the following skills can be said to develop from this ability. One cannot begin to approach learning the more advanced aspects of this art before one attains *sung*. If there are any "secrets" in Tai Chi, this is it. Not because it's difficult to understand but because it's very difficult to do. It is as much a mental activity as it is a physical one.

Tai Chi practitioners first embrace *sung* while practicing the solo form. As they move through the sequence of postures they start to become aware of where in their bodies they are rigid and holding tension. They observe how this rigidity can affect their balance. Discovering, refining, and making adjustments in relaxing the body is a major goal of the Tai Chi solo form. This promotes health and is a lifelong pursuit.

The practitioner encounters different difficulties when entering into the two-person exercises. It becomes much more complicated to maintain the desired *sung* when practicing with a partner than when exercising by oneself. This is because all sorts of psychological issues present themselves. The desire not to look awkward, the fear of getting hurt, the desire to control the outcome, the desire to compete and win, and so on are thoughts that distract the practitioner from relaxing and instead contribute to tensing of the muscles.

Such thoughts also distort and distract from your ability to perceive what is actually happening within the transactions of the movements. Instead of being able to understand what your partner is doing, your thoughts are somewhere else. It's analogous to talking to oneself while someone is trying to convey a subtle idea to you. You won't be able to hear what they are saying. It results in preconceived actions and judgments that are not based in present knowledge but instead on "gut" reaction.

One way to illustrate this is with a pushing exercise that I like to use when I give a workshop or demonstration. To be fair, it's a kind of parlor trick—but useful nonetheless. I begin by announcing to the audience that before the demo is over "I'll push someone without touching them." This always arouses people's curiosity, and I'll repeat my claim a few more times. But without anyone noticing, I'll change my wording from "I'll *push* someone" to "I'll *move* someone without touching them." Then I'll ask my arbitrarily picked participant to stand up in front of the group. I ask him or her to protect themselves by folding their arms in front of their chest, and then I'll ask some big strong people to stand a few paces behind to catch the person. When they are ready I move quickly toward my "victim" with my arms outstretched ready to push. Just short of touching them I abruptly stop and pull back. Invariably the "victim," thinking that they are about to be pushed backward, reacts in expectation by stiffening up and then falling forward. I, of course, then announce to the audience that I have made good on my claim that "I can make someone *move* without touching them."

This reaction is a good illustration of what happens internally when one reacts to an imagined stimulus. The body tenses and becomes rigid.

This is usually accompanied by an upward shift of the person's center of gravity (in Tai Chi this is called "floating"), creating an off-balance posture, which in my parlor trick results in the participant falling forward. All this happened simply because of something they were thinking. I didn't touch them, yet a preconception of an imagined push that never actually happened was enough to make the person fall forward.

"Learning How to Lose"

To correct this tendency to stiffen up and "float," the student is asked to embrace the idea of "learning how to lose" while practicing with a partner. This is not a morale-enhancing piece of advice but instead is an effective way to attain *sung*. It is a technique to help bypass all those preconceptions: the fear that someone will hurt you, the desires to compete, win, control, etc.

One simple exercise that specifically trains this is similar to my parlor trick. Two students face each other with both their right feet (or left) forward and opposite each other by about eighteen inches. One student will take the role of "pusher" and the other "pushee." The student who is pushing will limit his pushes (and pulls) to his partner's shoulder and chest area. The player who is getting pushed (who is the focus of this exercise) is asked to do absolutely nothing—to stay relaxed and let her partner push and pull her however he wants. She tries to not resist and not struggle but just allow herself to be pushed. Like a willow tree in the wind, she just yields to the pushes and pulls and if possible does not step out of position with her feet. To add to the unpredictability of what he is doing, the pusher will sometimes fake a push. This allows the partner who is getting pushed to observe her own reactions.

Within this non-competitive exercise you get to observe and become familiar with your fluctuating center of gravity and how your muscles tense up with a perceived push, real or fake. The attitude of losing and observing is what the Tai Chi practitioner carries with him as he interacts with a partner. With continued practice and familiarity with your internal dialogue, you gradually begin to quiet down and relax.

Learning how to lose is best described by the late modern-day Tai Chi teacher Cheng Man Ching's idea of "Quiet minding while investing in loss."

Investing in loss refers to letting go, to consciously make a decision to refrain from trying to control the movements or the outcome of the inter-action with a partner. *Quiet minding* refers to carefully watching and observing yourself as you let go and don't resist. You watch yourself stiffen and feel how your center of gravity rises as you encounter out-side stimulus. You don't close your eyes and give up but instead stay ever alert to (changing) possibilities. You also don't try to analyze and dissect every movement but instead observe the overall picture.

Now we can go back to the ideas behind the symbol of the Tai Chi and see how this "learning how to lose" applies. Inherent in the dynamic of yin and yang is the evolution of the hard into the soft (masculine into the feminine) and vice versa. There is a constant appearing and disap-pearing, enlarging and shrinking, that occurs in the perpetual transfor-mation of yin into its opposite, yang; and yang into yin.

This is a description of you and your partner's ever-changing move-ments. Some are coming at you. Some are moving away or moving up or down. Some movements are hard, some soft, some small, some large, and everything in between. To adapt to actions that are constantly in the throes of change, you adopt an attitude or posture of "losing." This entails refraining from categorizing or reducing your partner's movements down to the smallest parts.

There is far too much information to adapt to and keep track of all at once. Not only do you have to be aware of all the compound movements of your partner, but you also have to account for your own body—the angle and position of your joints and limbs as well as your weight dis-tribution, to say nothing of all the minute equations of inertia and force. How can you, rapidly and concurrently, comprehend and respond to all this?

While performing the two-person dance you do not try to focus on your partner's specific actions but instead consciously back off and let go in order to perceive a larger picture: a view of the whole structure. This permits you to be in a position to recognize the potential for latent movements in your partner, even when there is none apparent. This in turn opens up the possibility for *an informed action* as opposed to a blind *reaction.* It is analogous to creative insight where an artist, having spent years in preparation learning their craft, is open to a creative idea. Jazz musicians, "jamming" together, are a good example: immersed in the traditions and skills of their craft they are prepared for and open to "inspi-ration." Without rigidly adhering to a set pattern of notes, they are alert to the creative possibilities that present themselves. This requires an attitude that embraces chance and uncertainty.

Observation makes clear to the Tai Chi practitioner that there is some wisdom in allowing for this ambiguity, as it allows one to perceive multiple actions simultaneously. This is the nature of *sung*. It is the foundation of what I like to call the "Subtle Skills" of Tai Chi. Without its development and capacity, one can say that there is no Tai Chi Chuan.

All of the above ideas can be summed up with the simple Tai Chi statement: "Small loss, small gain. Big loss, big gain."

Chang Man Ching, with T.T. Liang, demonstrating Tai Chi in New York.

T.T. Liang with outdoor class, Botanical Gardens, Taiwan 1965.

6

The Subtle Skills

A good way of thinking about the more subtle aspects of this dance is to compare it to language. I recently heard a language specialist talking about how a culture's maturity is reflected through its use of language. When comparing "older" languages like Chinese or Arabic to "newer" ones like English, he described how one observes that words in older languages are more contextual, allowing more possibilities and subtleties of meaning. In newer cultures there is a seeming reliance on positions of extreme (black and white, good and evil, hard and soft) and little appreciation of the subtle gradations between them.

Arabic is an older language that allows for these gradations. There are, according to this speaker, some twelve words that convey different meanings and qualities of love. There is one word for the love of a grandparent to a grandchild, another for the love of two lovers, one for the love of family, and so on. In English, on the other hand, we have one all-purpose word, "love," that covers all qualities of love: You *love* your work, you *love* your wife, you *love* your spaghetti. . . .

This same idea of different qualities and gradations of meaning holds true with the language of movement and dance. There are more ways of looking at the transactions that take place between partners than simply a push and a pull. Every movement has different qualities and intentions. In Tai Chi, as in Arabic, there are different shades of understanding regarding the interactions that take place between partners. These are the subtle skills learned in order to differentiate, understand, and respond to both your own and your partner's movements.

Tai Chi does not emphasize the use of muscular strength, but instead supports the subtle and skillful employment of your strength and energy. You will continuously work to refine its use with the goal of expediting its implementation. To understand the subtleties of these refinements, different branches of skills (commonly translated from Chinese as *"energies"*) have been developed. The following is a look at a progression of six skills that one is training while practicing the two-person dance. They are:

1. Adhering
2. Listening
3. Interpreting
4. Neutralizing
5. Issuing
6. Receiving

It should be noted that the following are learned one after the other. Each skill depends on the preceding one to be successful. All are based on (and are a product of) the ideas contained within the concept of *sung*.

1. Adhering

"Adhering" contains the idea of both partners staying lightly attached to each other through every movement of the dance. Over time, with repetitive practice, the body will become sensitive to any advance or retreat so that there is never any loss of contact. You forget yourself, follow and adapt to all the changes your partner makes. Without resisting and without letting go, you follow the direction of your partner's force, advancing or retreating, and keep in delicate contact with every movement, whether straight, circular, large, or small.

Adhering includes advancing and retreating steps as well. Special attention is paid to the placement of your feet. You must locate and adjust them so that you can remain in an advantageous position toward your partner (in any situation).

When you have learned how to stay attached with a light sensitivity, you are then ready to develop the next skill: the ability to feel or "listen" to your partner's movements.

2. Listening

When engaging in a verbal conversation you have to be able to listen before you have the option to understand and respond. The same holds true while moving with your partner. In order to be able to interpret and make an informed action, you first have to be able to listen with your body to your partner's movements.

"Listening with your body" is an accurate description. Your ears pick up vibrations that you interpret as words. So too, your hands sense vibrations that you interpret as movements. Located within your skin, muscles, tendons, and joints are specialized cells called "mechanoreceptors" that are responsible for the monitoring of body movements and orientation by your brain—both consciously and unconsciously. The highest density of these receptors is found in the fingertips (and the tongue). This is the reason why one hand must always remain attached to your partner.

We spend a lot of time and effort, from infancy on, deciphering the nuances and quality of sounds in order to interpret them as words. We need to do the same with interpreting the nuances of movement stimulation. Over time, with continued practice and focus on tactile sensitivity, we can enlarge our "vocabulary" of understood movements.

One of the reasons why there is so much emphasis in Tai Chi on not resorting to or using external muscular force is that this impedes our ability to "listen." Tensing your muscles interferes with the signals sent to the brain from the mechanoreceptors. If we are involved in our own thoughts, we won't be able to hear accurately what is being said.

If we can relax, without allowing any defects of tension and rigidity (contraction equals constriction), we then have the option to "listen" to our partner. This in turn gives us the opportunity to be able to interpret their movements.

3. Interpreting

Interpreting is the ability to decipher the intent of your partner's movements and to adjust to them. It is the ability to comprehend their substantial and insubstantial aspects, their condition of balance, and whether they are floating, extending, sinking, etc.

If you cannot feel the location of your partner's center of gravity (root), it is akin to being blind. Any movement you make in response to your partner will be like a "blind man's bluff." You will be just guessing as to whether your responding action is correctly directed. This lack of sensitivity will in turn compel you to rely solely on external muscular force to affect your partner.

As you increase your ability to "interpret" you begin to comprehend degrees of nuance. This is described as first being able to perceive increments of feet, then inches, then tenths of inches, to thousands of an inch and beyond.

This corresponds to the circular movements you execute while engaging your partner. The finer the degree of your interpreting ability, the smaller your circular movements will become.

Stuart Alve Olson, in his book *The Intrinsic Energies of Tai Chi Chuan*, gives a very good description of three refined degrees of interpreting:

1) Sensing the Actualization. As the coarsest skill of interpreting, this is where you determine the physical movement of an incoming attack and then neutralize it. This is like seeing an arrow just as it is shot and being able to evade it.

2) Sensing the Inception. In this more refined application, you are able to sense an opponent's initial intent to draw in force in order to attack you, but you close it off before it is released. This is like seeing the arrow just as it is being drawn back in the bow and then stepping in and preventing the release of the arrow in the first place.

3) Sensing the Mind-Intention. In this, the highest aspect of interpreting, you are able to sense the intent in the opponent's eyes before he can physically express any action. Thus, you can choose to defeat the opponent before the bow is even raised — or, on the other extreme, allow the arrow to nearly reach your body before deflecting it.

4. Neutralizing

After you have attached to your partner and followed their movements, listened to and then interpreted their velocity and direction, you are now in a position to neutralize their potential effect. This means comprehending exactly the correct time to divert their incoming force away from your body to one side. The moment your partner's force is slightly extended or off-balance you direct it away from your own center of balance.

One example is when you let your partner push toward your center. You yield enough to make her commit to the intent of her push, and at that precise moment you divert it away from your center. Your partner then finds herself pushing nothing and her force completely neutralized. This is sometimes referred to as "open the door and let the robber in." It means that you expose your center to let your partner believe that there is an opportunity to push. When she has committed her force or "given you her energy" you then get out of the way. Timing is critical here. If you neutralize too early, her force will not have been committed and nothing will happen. If you neutralize too late, you will already have been pushed.

Another example of neutralizing is to follow your partner's force until it has dissipated. A good example of this is to imagine the movement of a large pendulum swinging toward you. While it is swinging it has the full force of its weight behind its movement. There is one point, though, where its weight and force have completely dissipated. That's when the swing has reached its furthest point and is just about to swing back in the other direction. Right at that moment, for a split second, the pendulum, in a sense, becomes weightless. If you have adhered and followed it to this point of its swing you have effectively neutralized its effect. It is also at this moment that you now have an opportunity to "issue."

The above examples introduce the Tai Chi technique "to neutralize means to attack." This is how you borrow your partner's energy and use it against them. When their incoming force has met no resistance, by being diverted or adhered to, and has reached its furthest point, it must, like the pendulum, pull back in order to regain its equilibrium. You now have the opportunity to use this pulling-back motion from your partner and add to it with your own force. In this sense your partner is participating and helping you with your push. I stress here *opportunity,* as you will only use it if the correct circumstances present themselves. In this sense the aforementioned Tai Chi saying "to neutralize means to attack" might translate as "to neutralize *gives the opportunity* to issue."

5. Issuing

When you become familiar with the movements of your partner and begin to acquire the skills of maintaining your position (central equilibrium), adhering without letting go, and the ability to interpret and neutralize incoming force, you are now ready to approach how to push your partner. This is commonly referred to as "issuing energy."

Prolonged Issuing: Strength and power can be generated through an intrinsic or tenacious use of the body rather than with external and often rigid muscular force. Using a whip or a rope as an example, it can be observed that although the length of the whip always remains limp, a powerful force can be generated through it, as displayed by the snapping "crack" of its tip.

Your body remains completely relaxed. Your sinews and tendons allow a wave motion to pass through them toward your partner. This wave motion is generated from your feet and legs, is directed by your waist, and issues through any part of your body, not necessarily your hands. If you do issue through your hands, the distance between them and your body before, during, and after the release of energy remains the same.

Abrupt Issuing: Liang described this to me as "similar to walking around with an atomic bomb: you can never use it!" This is the same wave motion described above except that the waves are much closer together. A better description of the wave would be vibration (the wave becomes a vibration). Imagine two wooden blocks resting next to each other. One is adhered to the floor while the other is free to move. If you took a hammer and hit the fixed block, the free block would move.

Another way of describing Abrupt Issuing is to look at the the Chinese Balls as an example. Everyone has seen the five steel balls that are suspended next to each other on a frame (see picture). When one of the end balls is allowed to swing and hit the remaining stationary balls, three of them will remain still but the ball on the other side will move outward in the opposite direction. When it swings back, it will affect the opposite end ball in the same way.

What is happening to the balls in the middle? They remain stationary yet a wave or vibration passes through them to expel the ball on the

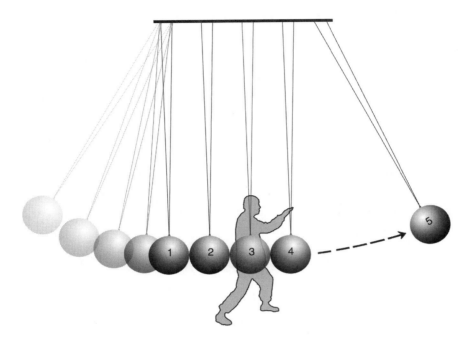

other side. This accurately describes Abrupt Issuing energy. The stationary ball in the middle is you. The vibration passing through is generated from your feet and legs and is directed by your waist toward your partner—the end ball.

In order for this vibration to function properly, it has to be focused in a directed line toward a single point. All the balls have to be lined up properly, one hitting the other in progression. Ball 1 hits ball 2 which hits ball 3 and so on. Likewise, this vibration travels through your body in a directed progression. If you move your hands before your feet, you will have disrupted the focus and force of the push.

Within the skill of issuing there are different characteristics as well. For example, sinking your weight as you issue downward will result in uprooting your partner. Using a spiral motion while issuing increases torque and will allow your energy to penetrate below the surface of what is being pushed.

6. Receiving

"Receiving" is a combination of the above five skills wrapped into one skill. It is the advanced ability to combine them all into one perceptible movement. As a result, if someone attempts to push you, he is immediately repulsed backward.

The previous five skills can be described in the turning motion of a circle. (See diagram.) The circling-back motion is adhering, interpreting, and neutralizing. The movement forward is to follow and, if possible, issue. The skill of receiving is to refine this circle to a point. It is still a circle, but the movements are brought so close together that they are imperceptible as separate movements and are best described as a single point. This is where what was once perceived in increments of feet is now understood within the tiniest fractions of an inch. The subtlest nuances of timing, direction, and circumstance are all thoroughly comprehended and acted upon in an instant.

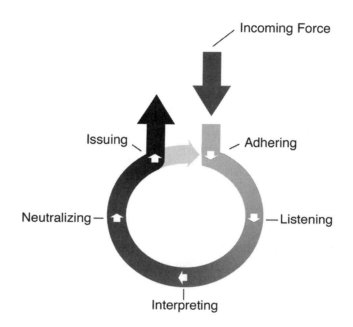

Correct Practice

The reason why students are asked to refrain from jumping ahead is that each skill depends on the previous one. You need to thoroughly understand one aspect before going ahead to the next. If you're thinking about neutralizing when you have not comprehended how to adhere and listen, your practice will devolve into mere "horse play." It may be fun, but it will increase your time of study.

In music, the deceptively free spirit of jazz musicians comes from a thorough comprehension of fundamental skills. Practice and repetition of basic scales is the first step and foundation of that freedom. Likewise, in Tai Chi, you should thoroughly master the first skill before going on to the next skill. This is accomplished by repeating the form over and over with your partner.

Inoch Yu and T.T. Liang performing "Golden Rooster Stands on One Leg" from the Two-Person Dance, Taiwan 1960.

7

Tai Chi Dance for the Martial Artist

After you have learned how to yield completely, you can begin to learn how to counter-attack. You will have to learn withdraw and attack techniques, folding techniques, how to find your opponent's defects and your own superior position, how to locate your opponent's center of gravity, how to concentrate on one point, how to avoid double-weighting, how to find the opponent's straight line, how to develop intrinsic energy while avoiding the use of external muscular force (a force from the bones). By constant vigorous practice done correctly in this manner, plus study and remembering, one can reach a stage of total reliance on the mind. Go gradually according to the right method: above all, learn these techniques correctly. When you have all these techniques indelibly in your mind, counter-attack is absolutely certain to be effective. If it is otherwise and these techniques are not in your mind, it will be mere blind attack.

— T.T. Liang from his book *T'ai Chi for Health and Self-Defense* (Vintage 1977)

In the study of Tai Chi you first learn it for health. When that is achieved you can then approach it for self-defense. The martial skills are derived from the health aspects of learning how to relax, focus and lowering your center of gravity to gain "central equilibrium." So when someone says they study Tai Chi for health, whether they know it or not, they are also preparing the foundations of the martial art as well.

In this book you can replace the word "partner" with "opponent." Your opponent is the tool with which you hone your mental capacities.

The self-defense aspects are for developing a kind of "mental accomplishment."

Lines

When you have acquired the skills of adhere, listen, interpret, neutralize, and issue and are interested in pursuing the martial aspects of the art, you will need to understand the concept of "lines."

In order for a push to be efficient and not just blindly striking out when you feel resistance ("like a blind man's bluff"), you have to be able to determine exactly where your opponent's center of gravity is located. Next, you need to establish the correct direction, or "line," across that center in which to issue force. When this is done correctly it takes very little effort to uproot your partner. It is this subtle understanding of balance that makes an experienced Tai Chi practitioner's push appear so effortless. Tai Chi classic texts describe this as the ability "to deflect the momentum of a thousand pounds with the trigger force of four ounces."

How can one possibly deflect the momentum of a thousand pounds coming toward you with only four ounces? This seems like a riddle with a trick answer. The probability is, if you try it, you'll most likely get squashed like a bug. It can be done, though. The key is being able to find the exact center of balance of that incoming thousand-pound force.

A sculptor friend demonstrated an example of this "center of balance" clearly to me. He was working on a NOVA project, trying to understand the mystery of how the ancient Egyptians raised their huge stone obelisks. In order to experiment, he had a 5' wide x 40' long piece of stone, carved into the shape of an obelisk, lying on its side in his barn. He asked me if I thought I could lift it up. My response, of course, was "no!" He then motioned for me to give it a try. When I went to the tip and lifted, to my amazement it rose up effortlessly. He had placed a block underneath the stone slab, exactly in the middle of its weight distribution: *at the stone's*

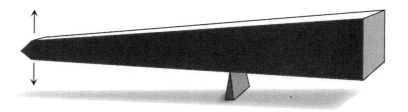

"center of balance." I could not move the stone to the right, left, or any other way but that particular up-and-down direction or line. And that only required the slightest amount of pressure (four ounces) for me to set it in motion.

To me this was a very clear description of the situation with my Tai Chi opponent. If I can detect and know where his exact center of gravity is, then I can find a specific line across it to issue force. He may be solid as a rock and many times my weight and strength, but if I can locate his center of balance and push across it he will move as easily as that stone obelisk.

Exposing a Defect Position

Your opponent will not necessarily cooperate with you in revealing his center. You have to learn how to recognize his ever-changing center of balance and determine the appropriate direction of your "line" of attack. There are as many possibilities of lines as there are variations that you and your opponent find yourselves in. (The Yang family reportedly categorized twenty-five of them.)

A good way to find and expose your opponent's center of balance is to bring him into what is called a "defect position." Think of your opponent as a low table resting on all four legs. In this position the table/your opponent is quite difficult to push over. The table's weight, distributed evenly on all four legs, is securely resting on the floor, and your (four-ounce) issuing force will have little effect. If your opponent moves, though, this is an entirely different matter. Once he is in motion you can then adhere/entice/maneuver your table/opponent up onto two legs where it becomes unstable, but it/he still has some stability between two legs. Now guide it up onto one leg where the table is tottering with all its weight on one point, in a "defect position" ready to fall. This is the position where the center of balance is exposed and where in Tai Chi one will

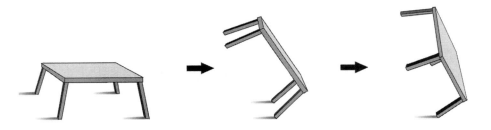

issue force. Four ounces of force will now be more than enough to fell the table/opponent.

A big problem with these examples is that your opponent is neither a table nor an obelisk. He is not rigid and immobile but instead is flexible, active, and mobile. This makes finding his center of gravity much more difficult. While you are adhering and moving with him, though, there are moments when his center of balance is exposed.

If you have thoroughly familiarized yourself with the previously discussed "skills" you will be able to lead your opponent into a defect position and then issue force in a line directed at the optimally effective angle and direction across his center. This opportunity to attack, though, lasts only for an instant. The more flexible your opponent is, the more difficult it will be to find his center of gravity and the closer your issuing line of force has to be to his center. With the obelisk, it was rigid so I could move it from the tip where my "line of force" was far from its center. If it were flexible, pushing on the tip would have had little or no effect.

Reviewing the posture of Roll Back in the Dance is a good way of summarizing all of the above principles. When your opponent's push is coming toward you, you *adhere* to him without resisting, *listen* to the quality of his push, *interpret* the direction and speed, and *neutralize* his force by directing him past your center where he, like the table on one leg, is now in a *defect position*. As he pulls back to regain his equilibrium, you use his energy to help you *issue* in a focused *line* directed across your opponent's *center of balance*.

This describes how an old man can accomplish quite remarkable feats in pushing. He does not rely on muscular force, but instead develops a conscious awareness of his opponent. This reliance solely on the mind is what is known in Tai Chi as "mental accomplishment."

8

The Two-Person Dance:
Posture Descriptions with Photographs

How to Make Sense
of the Following Posture Descriptions

Counts: Each posture is divided into 1 or 2 counts depending on its complexity. Each of these counts is divided into half beats. The movements within each half beat are explained. (Every "click" of the pictured metronome represents a half beat.)

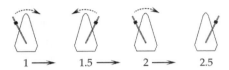

Photographs: For every posture there is a picture of T.T. Liang and his partner having completed that posture at the top of the page. Along the right side of the page is a sequence of pictures (starting at the top and moving downward) of two students demonstrating the counts of that posture. Each of these pictures represents a half beat and corresponds to the written description for it on the left side of the page.

View: The reader should view the photographs as though you are in the photograph yourself. You are on the page looking out ("north") and moving accordingly.

When reference is made to your waist or torso turning *clockwise* or *counter-clockwise* this is as if you are being viewed from above looking down on your movements.

Direction: For ease of explanation only, the four cardinal directions of north, south, east, and west are used so that you can orient yourself within the 360 degree circle that you will be performing the Tai Chi postures in. Where you are facing when you begin the exercises will become "north" (whether it actually is or is not does not matter). Each movement will be described in relationship to your chosen "north."

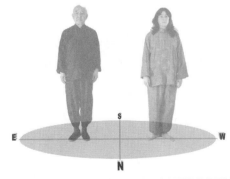

1. Opening Bow

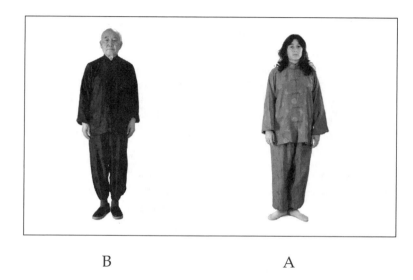

B   A

During the count of 2 beats:

A and B stand facing north with about 6 feet between them. Their heels are together and toes apart so that their feet form the letter "V." Their weight is distributed evenly between both feet and their arms hang loosely at their sides with palms facing in. Together, both bow forward to the north.

2. Opening Bow to Your Partner

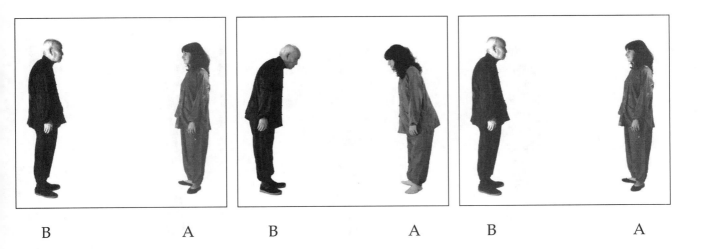

B   A   B   A   B   A

During the count of 2 beats:

A and B turn to face each other—again forming the letter "V" with their feet. Their hands remain relaxed at their sides. A and B then bow to each other.

3. Preparation

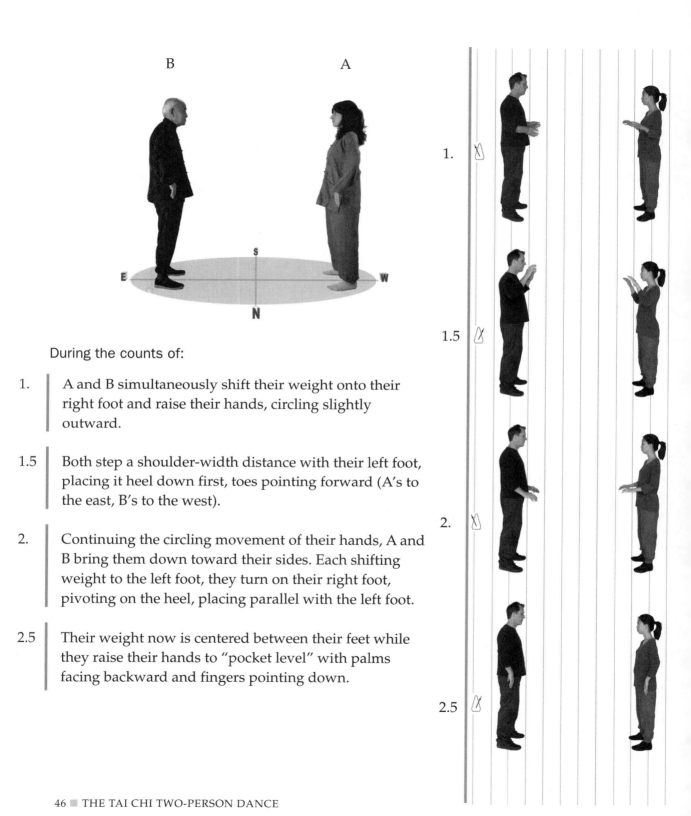

B　　　　　　　　　　A

During the counts of:

1. | A and B simultaneously shift their weight onto their right foot and raise their hands, circling slightly outward.

1.5 | Both step a shoulder-width distance with their left foot, placing it heel down first, toes pointing forward (A's to the east, B's to the west).

2. | Continuing the circling movement of their hands, A and B bring them down toward their sides. Each shifting weight to the left foot, they turn on their right foot, pivoting on the heel, placing parallel with the left foot.

2.5 | Their weight now is centered between their feet while they raise their hands to "pocket level" with palms facing backward and fingers pointing down.

1.

1.5

2.

2.5

Section 1

Postures 4–17

4. Step Forward and Chop

B   A

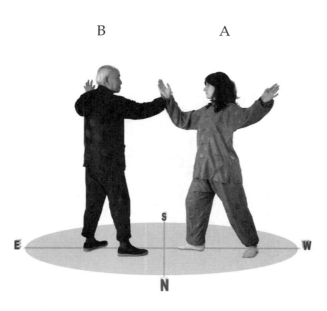

During the counts of:

1.	B takes a small step forward with his left foot to the south-west. At the same time he circles his left hand backward and counter-clockwise.
1.5	Shifting his weight onto his left foot, B steps forward with his right foot to the west and brings his right hand, forming a fist, to his left chest. His weight remains on the left leg.
2.	Pause ...
2.5	B then chops with his right fist to A's nose, keeping his weight back on his left leg. A receives the incoming fist by reaching out and "receiving" B's incoming chop with the back of her right hand and wrist and withdraws with it to stop its force. At the same time she steps back and out with her left foot, toes pointing north-east, and sinks her weight into her right front leg. Both A and B hold their back arms extended outward with their hands open and elbows slightly bent.

1.

1.5

2.

2.5

5. Roll Back (right style)

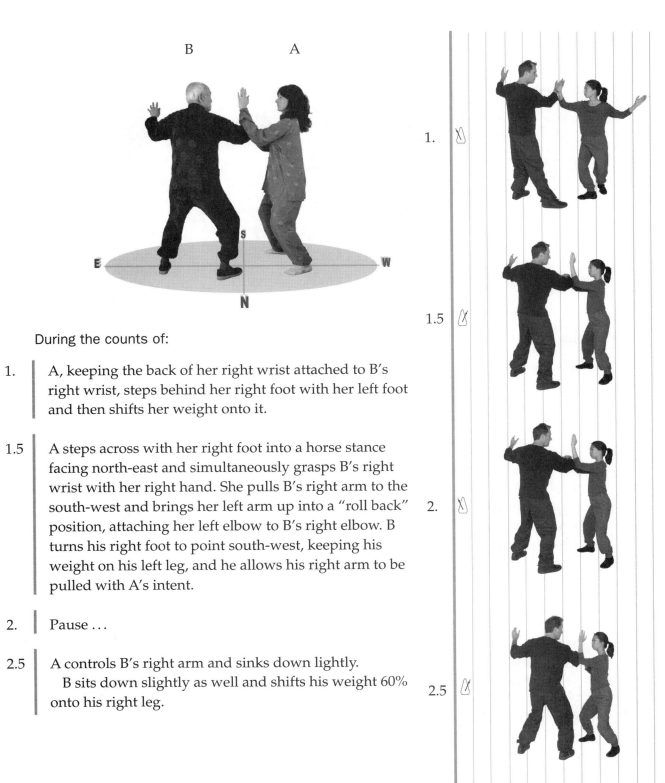

During the counts of:

1. A, keeping the back of her right wrist attached to B's right wrist, steps behind her right foot with her left foot and then shifts her weight onto it.

1.5 A steps across with her right foot into a horse stance facing north-east and simultaneously grasps B's right wrist with her right hand. She pulls B's right arm to the south-west and brings her left arm up into a "roll back" position, attaching her left elbow to B's right elbow. B turns his right foot to point south-west, keeping his weight on his left leg, and he allows his right arm to be pulled with A's intent.

2. Pause ...

2.5 A controls B's right arm and sinks down lightly.
   B sits down slightly as well and shifts his weight 60% onto his right leg.

6. Shoulder Stroke (right style)

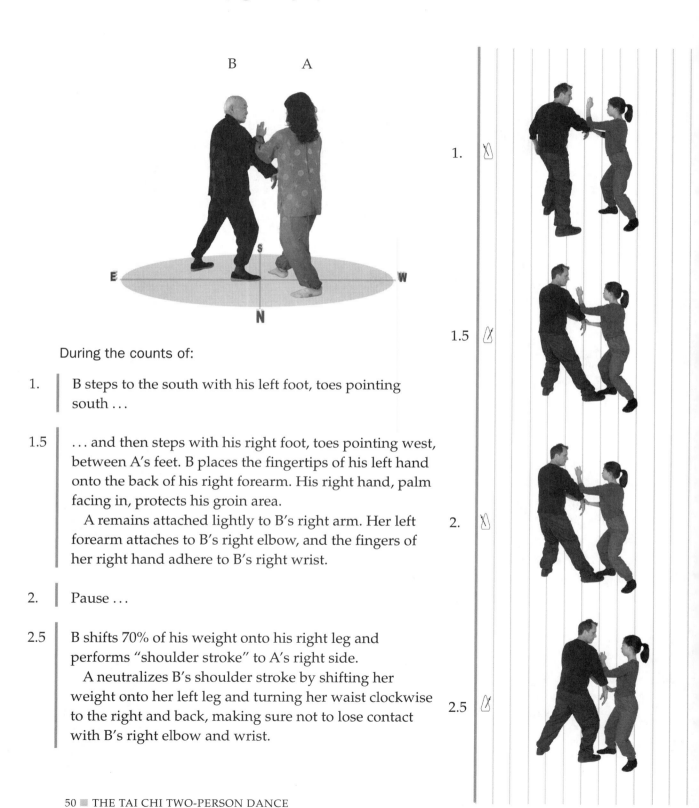

During the counts of:

1. | B steps to the south with his left foot, toes pointing south . . .

1.5 | . . . and then steps with his right foot, toes pointing west, between A's feet. B places the fingertips of his left hand onto the back of his right forearm. His right hand, palm facing in, protects his groin area.

    A remains attached lightly to B's right arm. Her left forearm attaches to B's right elbow, and the fingers of her right hand adhere to B's right wrist.

2. | Pause . . .

2.5 | B shifts 70% of his weight onto his right leg and performs "shoulder stroke" to A's right side.

    A neutralizes B's shoulder stroke by shifting her weight onto her left leg and turning her waist clockwise to the right and back, making sure not to lose contact with B's right elbow and wrist.

7. Slap (right style)

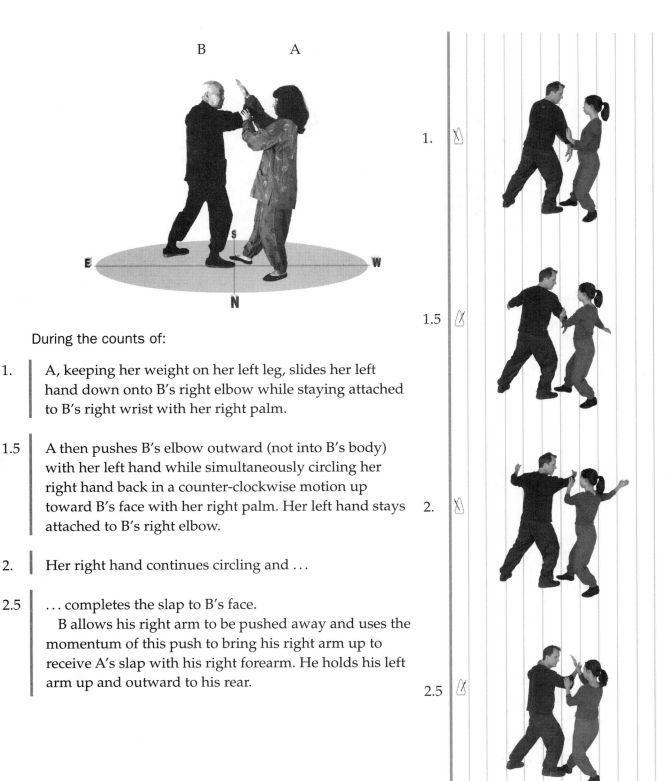

B   A

During the counts of:

1. | A, keeping her weight on her left leg, slides her left hand down onto B's right elbow while staying attached to B's right wrist with her right palm.

1.5 | A then pushes B's elbow outward (not into B's body) with her left hand while simultaneously circling her right hand back in a counter-clockwise motion up toward B's face with her right palm. Her left hand stays attached to B's right elbow.

2. | Her right hand continues circling and …

2.5 | … completes the slap to B's face.
B allows his right arm to be pushed away and uses the momentum of this push to bring his right arm up to receive A's slap with his right forearm. He holds his left arm up and outward to his rear.

8. Roll Back (right style)

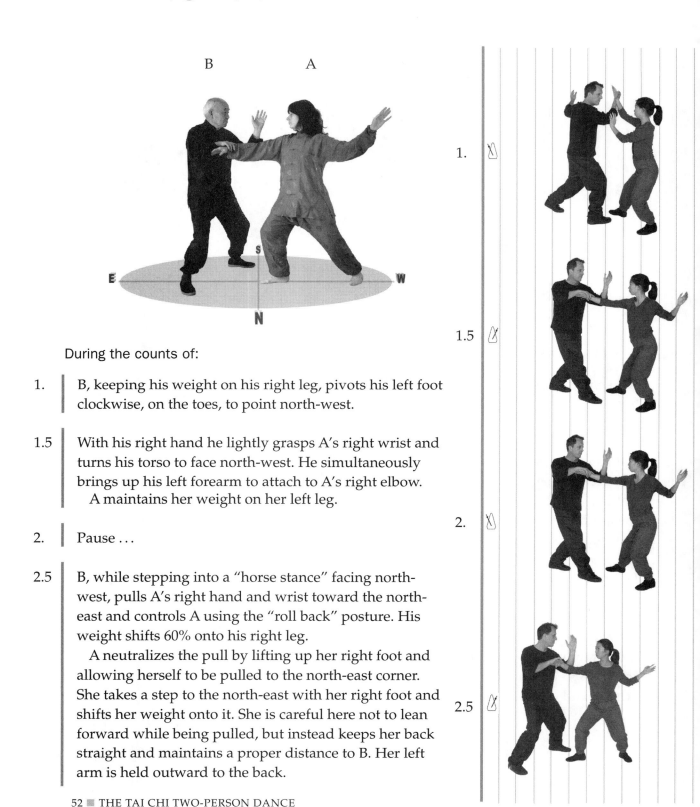

B   A

During the counts of:

1.	B, keeping his weight on his right leg, pivots his left foot clockwise, on the toes, to point north-west.
1.5	With his right hand he lightly grasps A's right wrist and turns his torso to face north-west. He simultaneously brings up his left forearm to attach to A's right elbow. A maintains her weight on her left leg.
2.	Pause ...
2.5	B, while stepping into a "horse stance" facing north-west, pulls A's right hand and wrist toward the north-east and controls A using the "roll back" posture. His weight shifts 60% onto his right leg. A neutralizes the pull by lifting up her right foot and allowing herself to be pulled to the north-east corner. She takes a step to the north-east with her right foot and shifts her weight onto it. She is careful here not to lean forward while being pulled, but instead keeps her back straight and maintains a proper distance to B. Her left arm is held outward to the back.

9. Shoulder Stroke (right style)

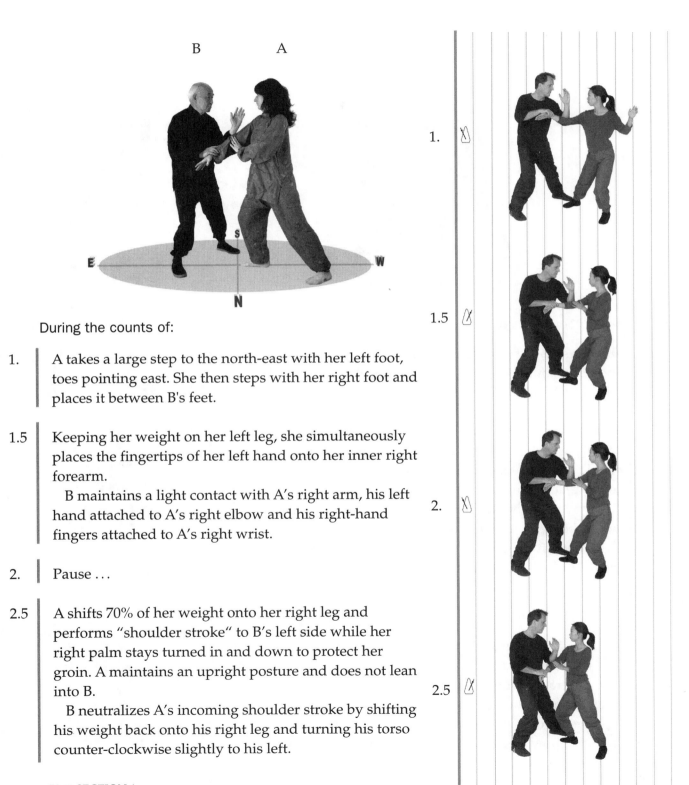

During the counts of:

1. | A takes a large step to the north-east with her left foot, toes pointing east. She then steps with her right foot and places it between B's feet.

1.5 | Keeping her weight on her left leg, she simultaneously places the fingertips of her left hand onto her inner right forearm.

   B maintains a light contact with A's right arm, his left hand attached to A's right elbow and his right-hand fingers attached to A's right wrist.

2. | Pause ...

2.5 | A shifts 70% of her weight onto her right leg and performs "shoulder stroke" to B's left side while her right palm stays turned in and down to protect her groin. A maintains an upright posture and does not lean into B.

   B neutralizes A's incoming shoulder stroke by shifting his weight back onto his right leg and turning his torso counter-clockwise slightly to his left.

10. Push

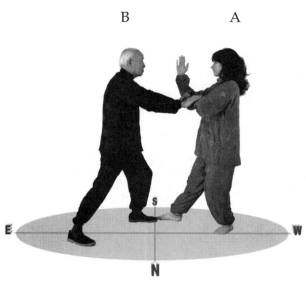

During the counts of:

1. | B places his left foot inside of A's right foot, toes pointing south-west. At the same time B attaches his left hand to A's left wrist.

1.5 | B then steps to the north-east with his right foot, toes pointing to the north-west, and shifts his weight to it while simultaneously attaching his right hand to A's left elbow. He is now facing A to the south-west. A follows B's movement but keeps her weight on her right leg while being careful not to lose contact with B's hands with her left forearm, which remains at chest level. Her right forearm attaches to B's left elbow.

2. | Pause ...

2.5 | B shifts 70% of his weight onto his left leg and pushes on A's left forearm.
    A neutralizes the incoming push by shifting her weight back onto her left leg and then turning her torso counter-clockwise to her left. Her right elbow attaches to B's left elbow as she turns her left palm up, her thumb turning over B's left wrist.

1.

1.5

2.

2.5

11. Roll Back (left style)

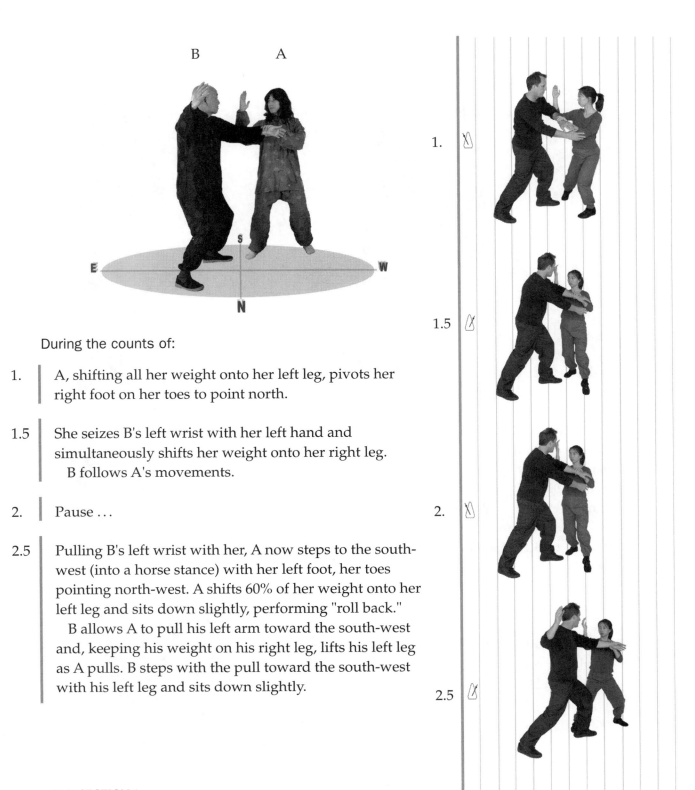

During the counts of:

1. | A, shifting all her weight onto her left leg, pivots her right foot on her toes to point north.

1.5 | She seizes B's left wrist with her left hand and simultaneously shifts her weight onto her right leg.
B follows A's movements.

2. | Pause ...

2.5 | Pulling B's left wrist with her, A now steps to the south-west (into a horse stance) with her left foot, her toes pointing north-west. A shifts 60% of her weight onto her left leg and sits down slightly, performing "roll back."
B allows A to pull his left arm toward the south-west and, keeping his weight on his right leg, lifts his left leg as A pulls. B steps with the pull toward the south-west with his left leg and sits down slightly.

12. Shoulder Stroke (left style)

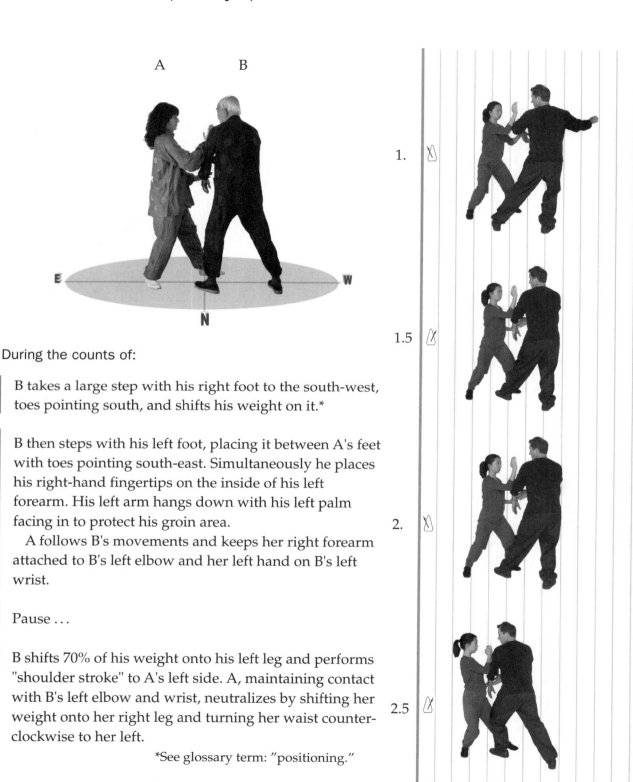

A   B

E

N

W

During the counts of:

1.	B takes a large step with his right foot to the south-west, toes pointing south, and shifts his weight on it.*
1.5	B then steps with his left foot, placing it between A's feet with toes pointing south-east. Simultaneously he places his right-hand fingertips on the inside of his left forearm. His left arm hangs down with his left palm facing in to protect his groin area. A follows B's movements and keeps her right forearm attached to B's left elbow and her left hand on B's left wrist.
2.	Pause ...
2.5	B shifts 70% of his weight onto his left leg and performs "shoulder stroke" to A's left side. A, maintaining contact with B's left elbow and wrist, neutralizes by shifting her weight onto her right leg and turning her waist counter-clockwise to her left.

*See glossary term: "positioning."

1.

1.5

2.

2.5

13. Slap (left style)

A   B

1.

1.5

2.

2.5

During the counts of:

1. | A, keeping her weight on her right leg, slides her right hand down onto B's left elbow while staying attached to B's left wrist with her left palm.

1.5 | She then pushes B's elbow outward with her right hand while simultaneously circling her left hand back in a clockwise motion up toward B's face with her left palm. Her right hand stays attached to B's left elbow.

2. | Her left hands continues circling and …

2.5 | … slaps to B's face.
B allows his left arm to be pushed away and uses this motion to bring his arm up to receive A's slap with his left forearm. His right arm is held outward to the back.

14. Roll Back (left style)

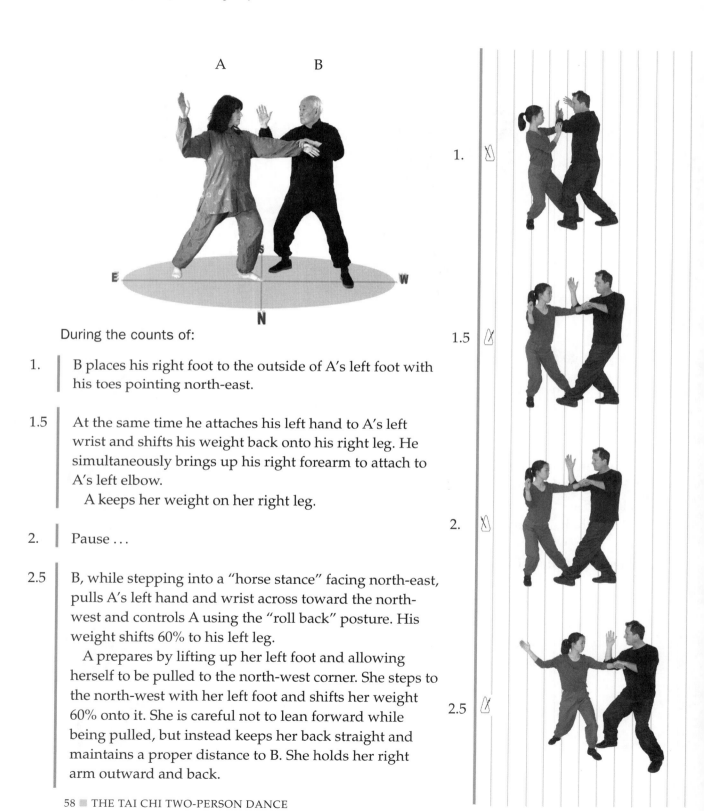

A   B

1.

1.5

2.

2.5

During the counts of:

1. | B places his right foot to the outside of A's left foot with his toes pointing north-east.

1.5 | At the same time he attaches his left hand to A's left wrist and shifts his weight back onto his right leg. He simultaneously brings up his right forearm to attach to A's left elbow.
    A keeps her weight on her right leg.

2. | Pause ...

2.5 | B, while stepping into a "horse stance" facing north-east, pulls A's left hand and wrist across toward the north-west and controls A using the "roll back" posture. His weight shifts 60% to his left leg.
    A prepares by lifting up her left foot and allowing herself to be pulled to the north-west corner. She steps to the north-west with her left foot and shifts her weight 60% onto it. She is careful not to lean forward while being pulled, but instead keeps her back straight and maintains a proper distance to B. She holds her right arm outward and back.

15. Shoulder Stroke (left style)

A   B

1.

1.5

2.

2.5

During the counts of:

1.	A takes a large step to the north-west with her right foot, toes pointing north-west, and then steps with her left foot to the south-west, placing it between B's feet.
1.5	Keeping her weight on her right leg, she places her right-hand fingertips onto her inner left forearm. Her left arms hangs down with her palm turned facing the groin (to protect it). B maintains a light contact with A's left arm. His inner right forearm/elbow is attached to A's left elbow, his left-hand fingers lightly grasping A's left wrist.
2.	Pause ...
2.5	A shifts 70% of her weight onto her left leg and performs "shoulder stroke" to B's right side. She maintains an upright posture and does not lean into B. B neutralizes A's incoming shoulder stroke by shifting his weight onto his left leg and turning his torso slightly clockwise to his right.

16. B: Push
A: Withdraw Body and Roll Back

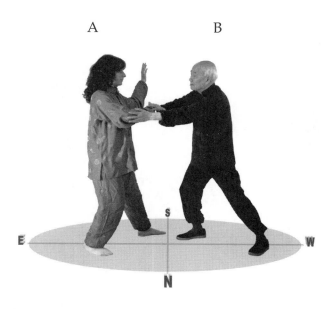

A   B

1.

1.5

2.

2.5

During the counts of:

1.	B places his right foot inside to the north of A's left foot, toes pointing east. At the same time B attaches his right hand to A's right wrist.
1.5	B then steps back to the north-west with his left foot, toes pointing to the north-east, and shifts his weight onto it. He simultaneously attaches his left hand to A's right elbow. B is now facing A to the east. A follows B's movement, but keeps her weight on her left leg while being careful not to lose contact with B's hands with her right forearm, which remains at chest level. Her left elbow attaches to B's right elbow.
2.	Pause . . .
2.5	B shifts 70% of his weight onto his right leg and pushes on A's right forearm. A neutralizes the incoming push by shifting her weight back onto her right leg and then turning her torso clockwise to her right. Her left elbow attaches to B's right elbow as she turns her right palm up, her thumb turning over B's right wrist.

17. Join Hands

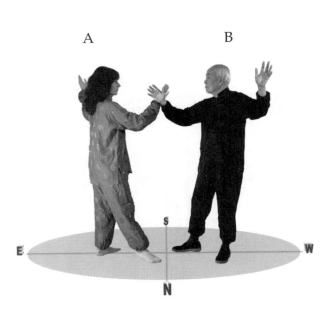

A   B

During the counts of:

1. | A steps back with her left foot and, shifting all her weight onto it, . . .

1.5 | . . . she then steps forward to the west with her right foot, placing it toe down, heel up.
    B, picking up his left foot, adjusts it a little forward or backward according to A's position, then shifting his weight onto it, places his right foot, with the toes touching the floor and the heel up, in front of and to the south side of A's right foot.

2. | A and B lightly join the backs of their right wrists together . . .

2.5 | . . . and simultaneously raise them up to eye level and bring their toes closer together—about 6 inches between them from north to south. Both A and B hold their left arms up and out.

This ending position is called "Join Hands" and will now be referred to as such.

1.

1.5

2.

2.5

Section 2

Postures 18–27

18. Step Forward and Punch

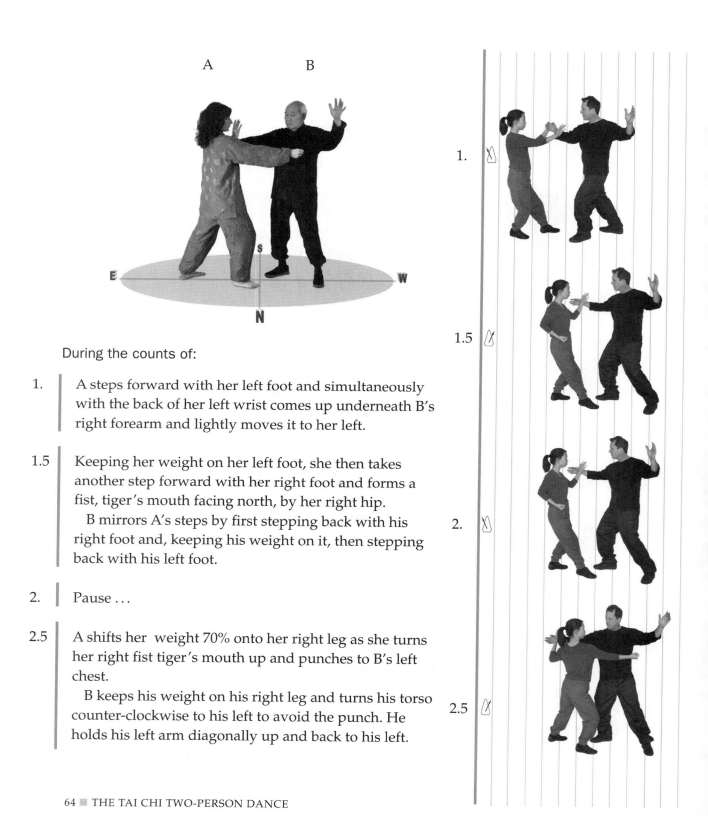

A   B

E
S
W
N

During the counts of:

1. A steps forward with her left foot and simultaneously with the back of her left wrist comes up underneath B's right forearm and lightly moves it to her left.

1.5 Keeping her weight on her left foot, she then takes another step forward with her right foot and forms a fist, tiger's mouth facing north, by her right hip.
   B mirrors A's steps by first stepping back with his right foot and, keeping his weight on it, then stepping back with his left foot.

2. Pause . . .

2.5 A shifts her weight 70% onto her right leg as she turns her right fist tiger's mouth up and punches to B's left chest.
   B keeps his weight on his right leg and turns his torso counter-clockwise to his left to avoid the punch. He holds his left arm diagonally up and back to his left.

1.

1.5

2.

2.5

19. Deflect and Chop

A   B

During the counts of:

1.	B picks up his left foot and puts it back down turned out, adjusting it according to A's position. At the same time he lightly grasps A's right wrist with his left hand …
1.5	… while bringing the right hand over to his left breast, forming a fist (palm down), and shifts his weight onto his left leg. A lightly adheres with her left hand, palm up, to B's right elbow and follows B's movements.
2.	Pause …
2.5	B chops with his right fist to A's forehead and then shifts his weight onto the right leg. He opens his fist after the chop. A neutralizes the incoming chop by shifting her weight onto her back left leg while leaning back and pushing up with her left hand under B's right elbow and throwing her head back. Her right hand can also be thrown back (as in posture #24).

1.

1.5

2.

2.5

20. Step Forward and Shoulder Stroke

A   B

During the counts of:

1.	A keeps control of B's right elbow with her left hand and pushes it upward and away while placing her right foot perpendicular, toes pointing north, in front of B's right foot (forming a "T").
1.5	A steps with her left foot, toes pointing west, to B's right side. B follows A's movements and waits to see how to neutralize.
2.	Pause ...
2.5	A then shifts her weight 70% onto her left foot and strikes with her left shoulder to the back of B's shoulder. B neutralizes by shifting his weight back onto his left leg and turns his torso clockwise to his right.

1.

1.5

2.

2.5

21. Withdraw Step and Strike Tiger

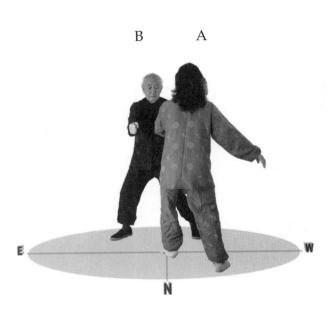

B   A

During the counts of:

1. | B adheres to A's left elbow with his left hand, fingers pointing up.

1.5 | B withdraws his right hand down to his right hip, forming it into a fist, palm up, and simultaneously withdraws his right foot a half-step back.

2. | B places his right foot, toes pointing east, three inches to the south side of A's left foot.
  A, in response, withdraws her left foot, placing it a half step to the north.

2.5 | B takes a step with his right foot to the east and strikes out to A's left side. He then shifts his weight onto his right foot while trailing his left foot around to the south, mirroring A's neutralizing movement.
  A takes a small step to the west with her left foot and then shifts her weight onto it and pivots on it, trailing her right leg around as she turns her torso to face south.

22. Elbow Stroke

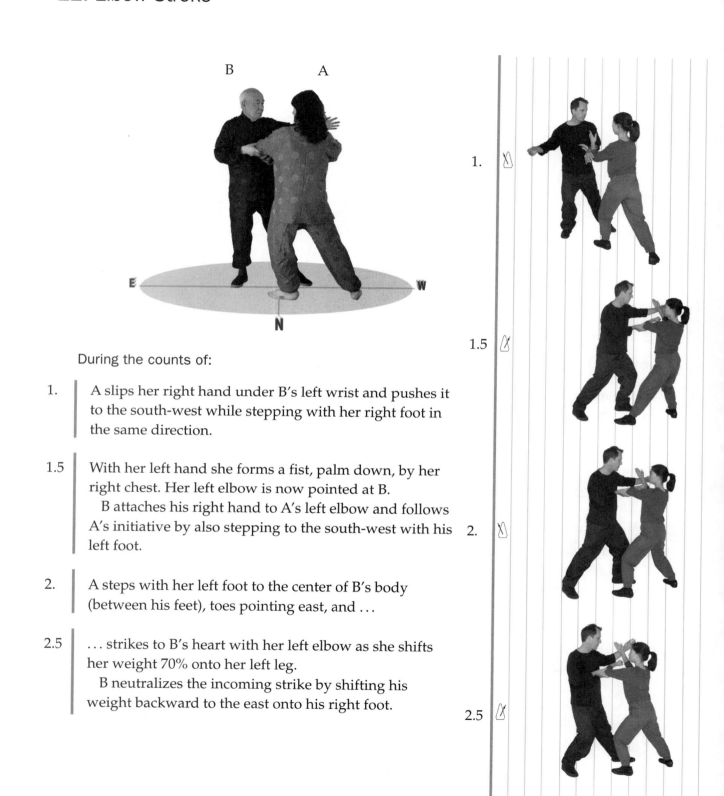

B   A

E   W

N

During the counts of:

1. | A slips her right hand under B's left wrist and pushes it to the south-west while stepping with her right foot in the same direction.

1.5 | With her left hand she forms a fist, palm down, by her right chest. Her left elbow is now pointed at B.
B attaches his right hand to A's left elbow and follows A's initiative by also stepping to the south-west with his left foot.

2. | A steps with her left foot to the center of B's body (between his feet), toes pointing east, and ...

2.5 | ... strikes to B's heart with her left elbow as she shifts her weight 70% onto her left leg.
B neutralizes the incoming strike by shifting his weight backward to the east onto his right foot.

1.

1.5

2.

2.5

23. Push with Right Hand

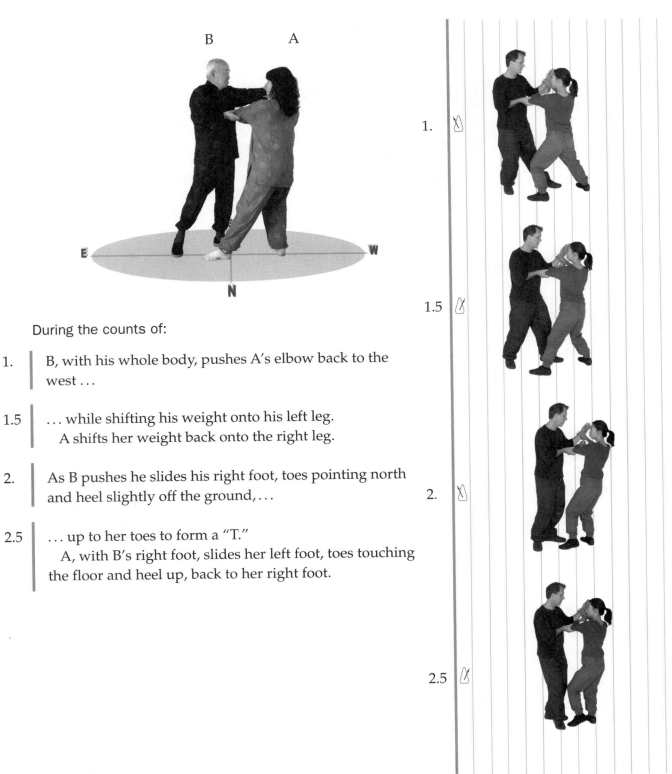

B   A

E   W

N

1.

1.5

2.

2.5

During the counts of:

1. | B, with his whole body, pushes A's elbow back to the west . . .

1.5 | . . . while shifting his weight onto his left leg.
A shifts her weight back onto the right leg.

2. | As B pushes he slides his right foot, toes pointing north and heel slightly off the ground, . . .

2.5 | . . . up to her toes to form a "T."
A, with B's right foot, slides her left foot, toes touching the floor and heel up, back to her right foot.

24. Chop with Fist

During the counts of:

1. | A steps forward with her left foot to the east, leading with her left elbow pointing to B's chest.
    B steps back with his right foot.

1.5 | A places her left foot between B's feet.
    B shifts his weight back onto his right foot.

2. | A unfolds her left arm...

2.5 | ... and chops to B's forehead with the back of her left fist. She then shifts her weight 70% onto her left leg.
    B neutralizes the incoming chop by leaning back and pushing up on A's left elbow with his right hand. He also throws his head and left arm back to avoid A's unfolding fist.

1.

1.5

2.

2.5

25. Shoulder Stroke (right style)

B   A

E ———————————— W

N

1.

1.5

2.

2.5

During the counts of:

1.	B keeps control of A's left elbow with his right hand and pushes it upward and away while placing his left foot perpendicular, toes pointing south, to A's left foot (forming a "T").
1.5	B steps with his right foot, toes pointing west, to A's left side. A follows B's movements and waits to see how to neutralize.
2.	Pause ...
2.5	B then shifts 70% of his weight onto his right leg and strikes with his right shoulder to the back of A's shoulder. A neutralizes by shifting her weight back onto her right leg and turning her torso counter-clockwise to her left.

26. Withdraw, Step, and Strike Tiger (left style)

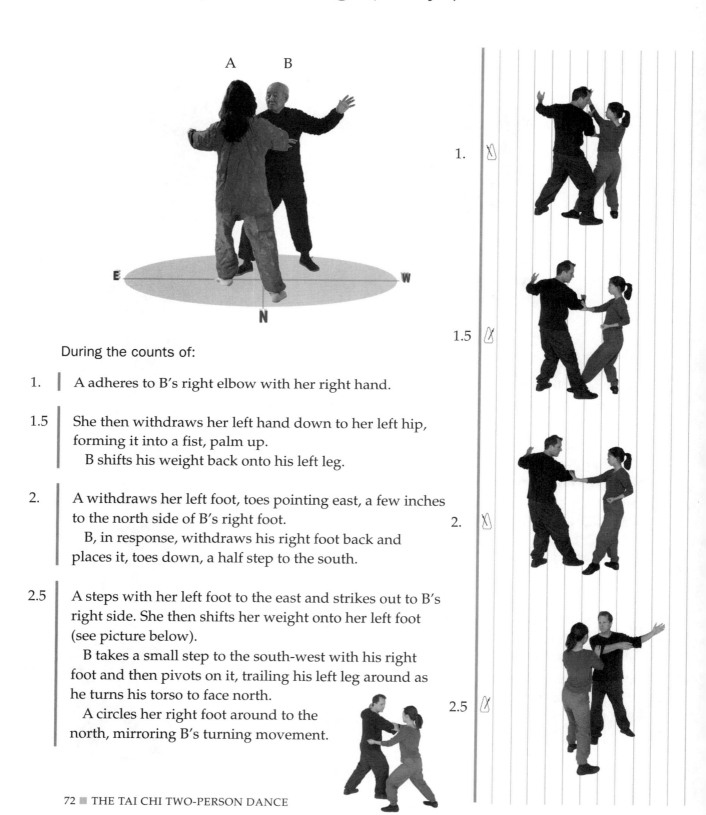

During the counts of:

1. | A adheres to B's right elbow with her right hand.

1.5 | She then withdraws her left hand down to her left hip, forming it into a fist, palm up.
　B shifts his weight back onto his left leg.

2. | A withdraws her left foot, toes pointing east, a few inches to the north side of B's right foot.
　B, in response, withdraws his right foot back and places it, toes down, a half step to the south.

2.5 | A steps with her left foot to the east and strikes out to B's right side. She then shifts her weight onto her left foot (see picture below).
　B takes a small step to the south-west with his right foot and then pivots on it, trailing his left leg around as he turns his torso to face north.
　A circles her right foot around to the north, mirroring B's turning movement.

27. Chop with Fist and Join Hands

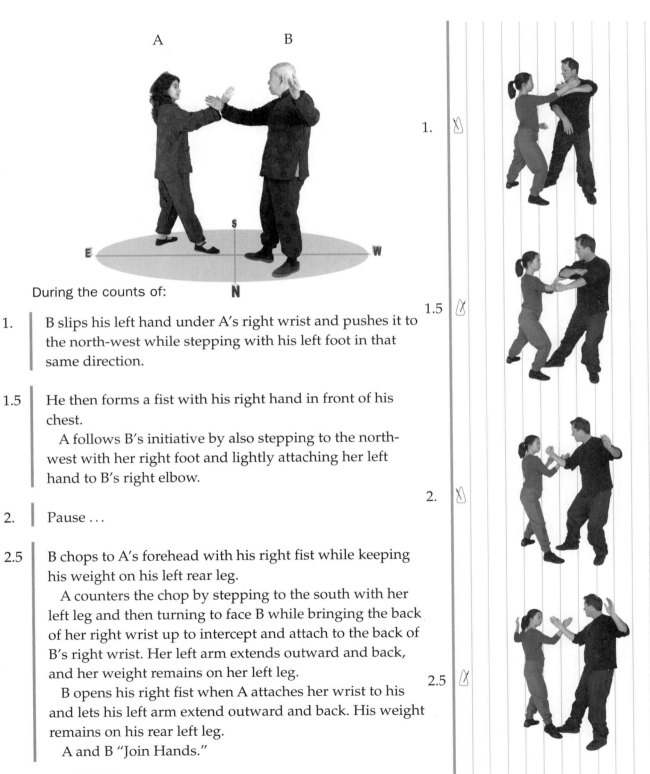

A   B

S
E   W
N

During the counts of:

1.	B slips his left hand under A's right wrist and pushes it to the north-west while stepping with his left foot in that same direction.
1.5	He then forms a fist with his right hand in front of his chest. A follows B's initiative by also stepping to the north-west with her right foot and lightly attaching her left hand to B's right elbow.
2.	Pause ...

2.5	B chops to A's forehead with his right fist while keeping his weight on his left rear leg.
	    A counters the chop by stepping to the south with her left leg and then turning to face B while bringing the back of her right wrist up to intercept and attach to the back of B's right wrist. Her left arm extends outward and back, and her weight remains on her left leg.
	    B opens his right fist when A attaches her wrist to his and lets his left arm extend outward and back. His weight remains on his rear left leg.
	    A and B "Join Hands."

1.

1.5

2.

2.5

Section 3

Postures 28–36

28. Block and Punch Upward

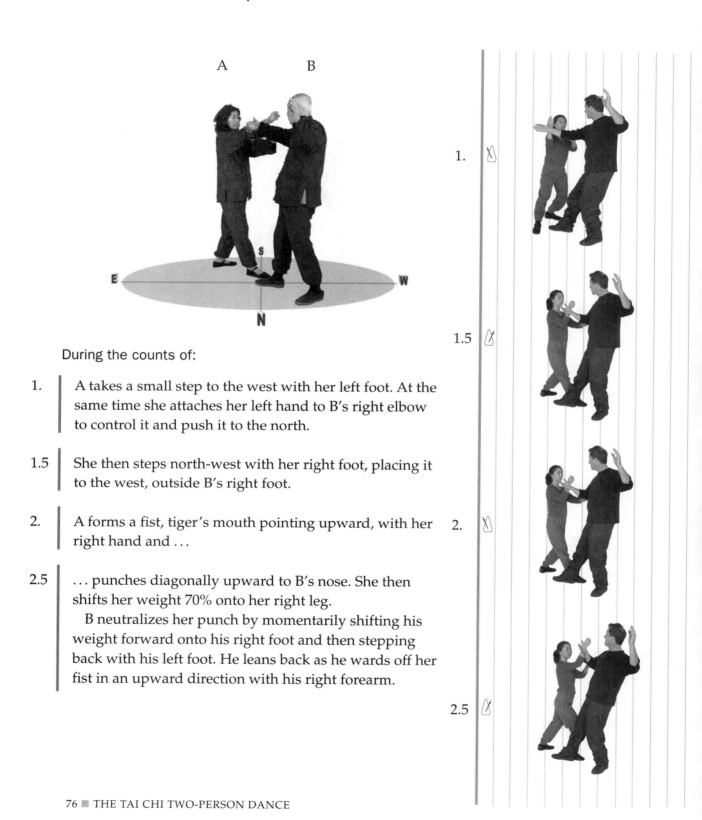

A   B

During the counts of:

1.   A takes a small step to the west with her left foot. At the same time she attaches her left hand to B's right elbow to control it and push it to the north.

1.5   She then steps north-west with her right foot, placing it to the west, outside B's right foot.

2.   A forms a fist, tiger's mouth pointing upward, with her right hand and ...

2.5   ... punches diagonally upward to B's nose. She then shifts her weight 70% onto her right leg.

     B neutralizes her punch by momentarily shifting his weight forward onto his right foot and then stepping back with his left foot. He leans back as he wards off her fist in an upward direction with his right forearm.

29. Turn Body and Push

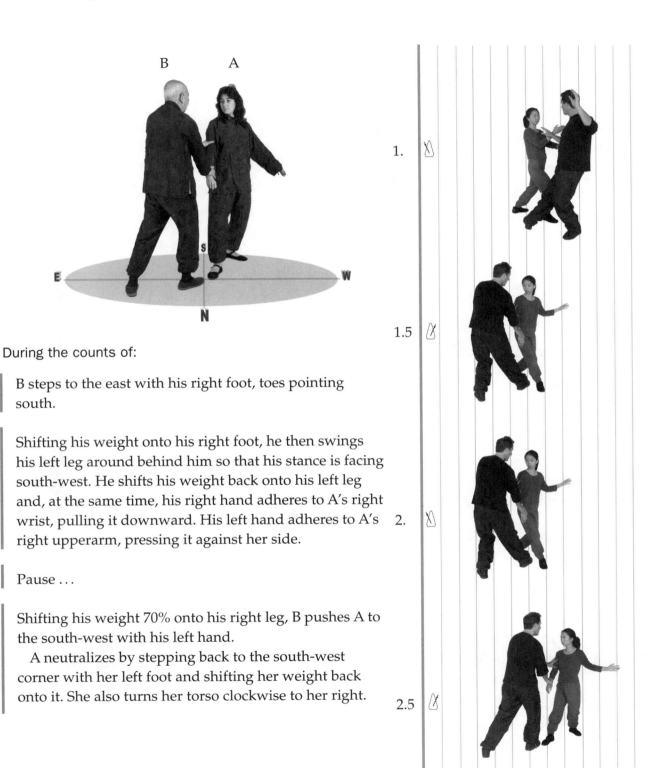

B   A

During the counts of:

1. | B steps to the east with his right foot, toes pointing south.

1.5 | Shifting his weight onto his right foot, he then swings his left leg around behind him so that his stance is facing south-west. He shifts his weight back onto his left leg and, at the same time, his right hand adheres to A's right wrist, pulling it downward. His left hand adheres to A's right upperarm, pressing it against her side.

2. | Pause . . .

2.5 | Shifting his weight 70% onto his right leg, B pushes A to the south-west with his left hand.
    A neutralizes by stepping back to the south-west corner with her left foot and shifting her weight back onto it. She also turns her torso clockwise to her right.

1.

1.5

2.

2.5

30. Fold and Chop with Fist

B   A

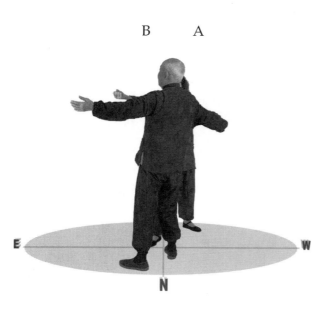

E   W

N

During the counts of:

1.	A picks up her left foot and, according to B's position, places it back down approximately where it was and ...
1.5	... circles over the top of B's right wrist with her left hand to move it out of the way toward the west. With her right hand she forms a fist, palm down, at her left chest and shifts her weight 90% onto her left leg.
2.	A steps forward with her right foot to the north-east ...
2.5	... and chops with the back of her right fist to B's forehead. She then shifts her weight 70% onto her right leg. B gets out of the way of the incoming chop by turning his waist counter-clockwise to his left.

1.

1.5

2.

2.5

31. Deflect and Punch

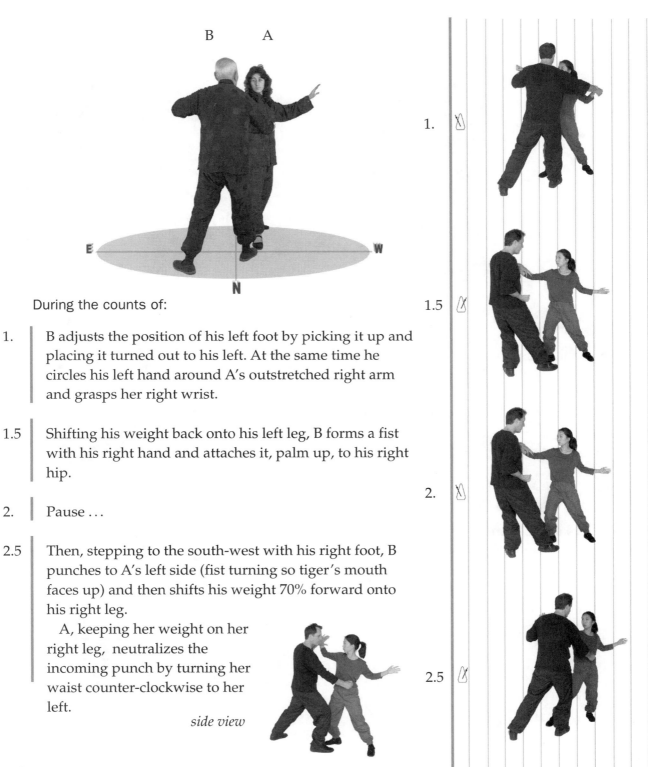

B   A

E   W

N

During the counts of:

1. | B adjusts the position of his left foot by picking it up and placing it turned out to his left. At the same time he circles his left hand around A's outstretched right arm and grasps her right wrist.

1.5 | Shifting his weight back onto his left leg, B forms a fist with his right hand and attaches it, palm up, to his right hip.

2. | Pause . . .

2.5 | Then, stepping to the south-west with his right foot, B punches to A's left side (fist turning so tiger's mouth faces up) and then shifts his weight 70% forward onto his right leg.

    A, keeping her weight on her right leg, neutralizes the incoming punch by turning her waist counter-clockwise to her left.

side view

1.

1.5

2.

2.5

32. Horizontal Split

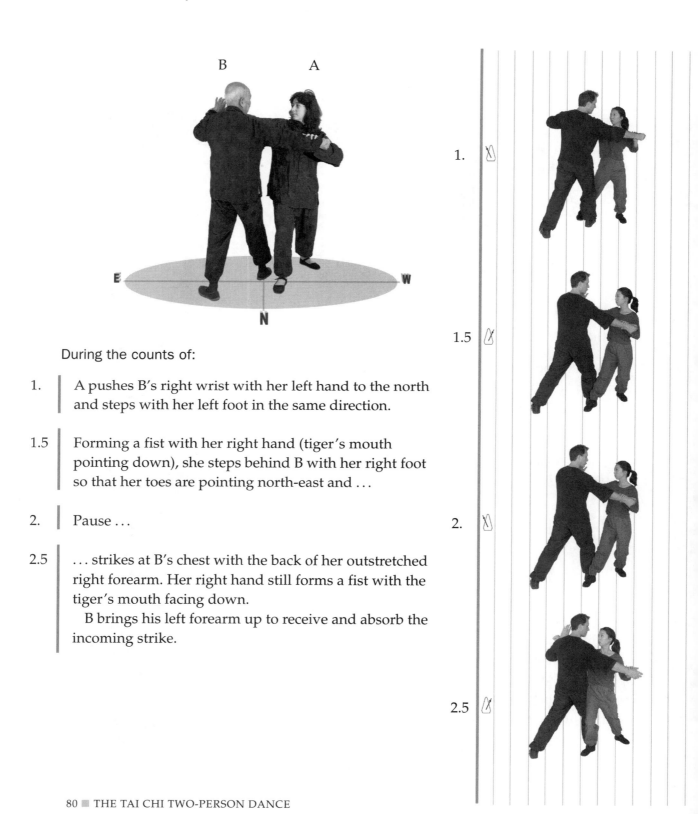

B   A

E   W

N

During the counts of:

1. | A pushes B's right wrist with her left hand to the north and steps with her left foot in the same direction.

1.5 | Forming a fist with her right hand (tiger's mouth pointing down), she steps behind B with her right foot so that her toes are pointing north-east and . . .

2. | Pause . . .

2.5 | . . . strikes at B's chest with the back of her outstretched right forearm. Her right hand still forms a fist with the tiger's mouth facing down.

B brings his left forearm up to receive and absorb the incoming strike.

1.

1.5

2.

2.5

33. Change Step and Parting Wild Horse's Mane (left style)

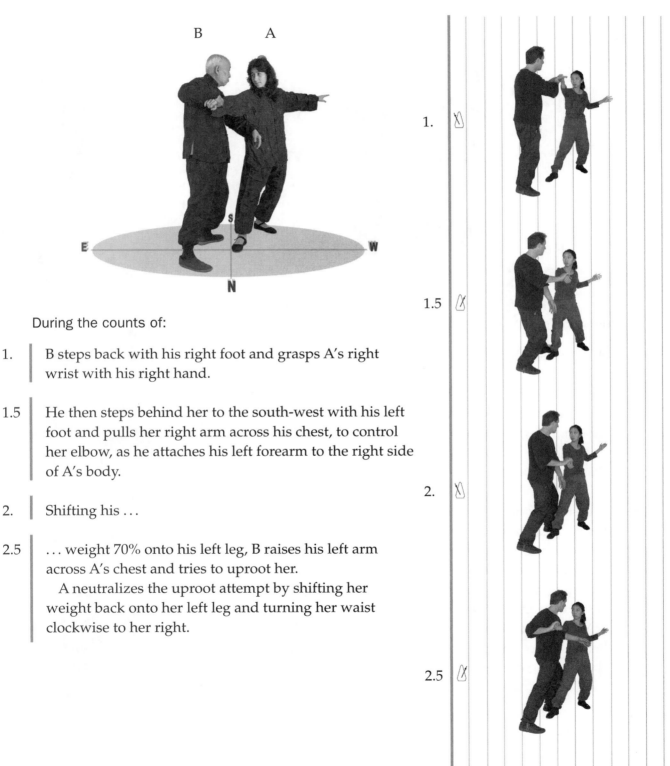

B   A

E   W
S
N

During the counts of:

1. | B steps back with his right foot and grasps A's right wrist with his right hand.

1.5 | He then steps behind her to the south-west with his left foot and pulls her right arm across his chest, to control her elbow, as he attaches his left forearm to the right side of A's body.

2. | Shifting his . . .

2.5 | . . . weight 70% onto his left leg, B raises his left arm across A's chest and tries to uproot her.
       A neutralizes the uproot attempt by shifting her weight back onto her left leg and turning her waist clockwise to her right.

1.

1.5

2.

2.5

34. Strike Tiger (right style)

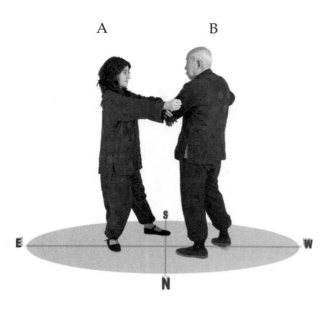

A   B

1.

1.5

2.

2.5

During the counts of:

1.	A attaches to B's left elbow with her left palm.
1.5	She withdraws her right foot and right hand at the same time. Her right hand forms a fist, palm up with tiger's mouth facing south, at her right hip.
2.	Pause . . .

2.5	A then steps outside of B to the east and punches with her right fist to B's left kidney.
	
	   B neutralizes by taking a small step to the west with his left foot and then pivots counter-clockwise on it, swinging his right leg around until he is facing south-east. He keeps his weight on his left leg.
	
	   A mirrors B's motion after her punch by pivoting on her right foot and letting her left leg swing around until she is facing north-west.

35. Turn Body, Withdraw, Step, and Roll Back

During the counts of:

1. B places the ball of his right foot near A's left foot while grasping A's left wrist with his left hand.

1.5 B then pivots on his right foot and swings his left foot around, ending up in a "horse stance" facing northwest. At the same time he attaches the inside of his right elbow to A's left elbow. . . .

2. Pause . . .

2.5 . . . and applies "roll back" to A by turning his waist to the left and locking A's left arm with his right elbow and left wrist.

   A neutralizes by sitting down slightly and rotating her arm counter-clockwise so that her elbow joint cannot be "locked."

36. Join Hands

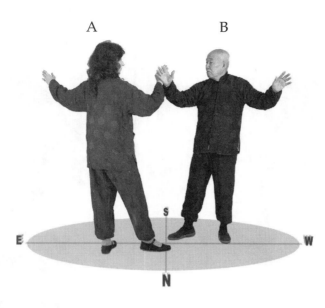

A   B

During the counts of:

1.	A picks up her left foot, turns her toes to point south, and places it back down in front of B's right foot.
1.5	She then attaches the back of her right wrist to B's right wrist (to protect her face).
2.	A shifts her weight onto her left foot and …

2.5	… then brings her right foot forward toward B, to the south-west, placing it "toes down heel up," and attaches the back of her right wrist to the back of B's right wrist—rising into the posture of "Join Hands."
	
	   B steps back with his left foot to adjust his position to A and, shifting his weight onto it, comes up into the "Join Hands" posture with A.
	
	   A is now facing south-west and B is facing north-east.

1.

1.5

2.

2.5

Section 4
Postures 37–50
Talu

37. Pull / Ward Off

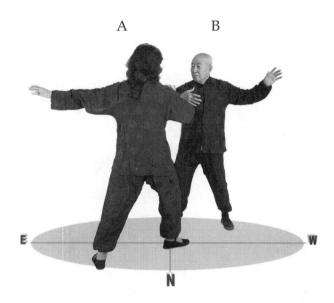

During the count of:

1.

A steps forward to the south-west corner with her right foot and attempts to grab B's right wrist.

B steps back with his left foot and wards off with his right hand, bringing his arm rounded out in front of him with his right palm facing his chest.

A's attempt to grab B's wrist having been effectively neutralized, she does not try to complete it. Instead she just stays attached to B's right wrist with her right hand.

38. Split / Roll Back

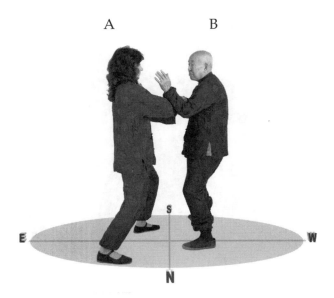

During the count of:

1.

A steps forward to the south-west with her left foot and grabs B's right wrist with her right hand. At the same time she reaches over with her left hand and places it under B's right elbow in an attempt to "split" it by pushing down with her right hand and up with her left.

B neutralizes by stepping back with his right foot and turning his torso clockwise to his right while simultaneously attaching his left elbow to A's right elbow. He brings his right palm up over A's left wrist.*

*This simple maneuver prevents A from grabbing his right wrist (see detail below— side view).

39. Elbow Stroke

During the count of:

1.

A steps forward to the south-west with her right foot and, folding her right arm, strikes to B's chest with her right elbow. She cups her left palm over her right fist to give her striking elbow support. *See detail below.

B steps back with his left foot and protects himself by holding A's striking elbow with his left hand as he shifts his weight onto his back leg to neutralize the incoming strike. He keeps his right hand lightly attached to A's right wrist.

opposite view

40. Push

During the count of:

B shifts his weight onto his right foot and pushes A's elbow with his left hand, keeping his right hand attached to her right wrist.

1.

A neutralizes B's push by letting her right arm collapse (straighten out) and shifting her weight back onto her left leg.

41. Shoulder Stroke

A   B

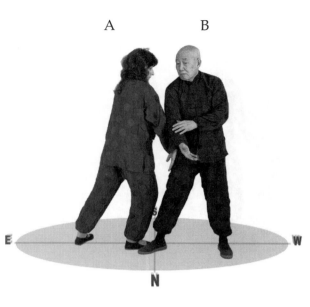

During the counts of:

1.   A steps to the south, outside B's right foot, with her right foot.

1.5   She then steps with her left foot around so she is facing B to the west.

2.   Pause . . .

2.5   Shifting 70% of her weight forward onto her right foot, A executes shoulder stroke to the right side of B's body. Her right arm is straight down with palm facing in, and her left hand lightly touches on the inside of her right forearm.

     B, making sure to maintain contact with A with his left hand on her elbow, neutralizes by shifting his weight back onto his left leg and turning his waist counter-clockwise, slightly to his right.

1.

1.5

2.

2.5

42. Press

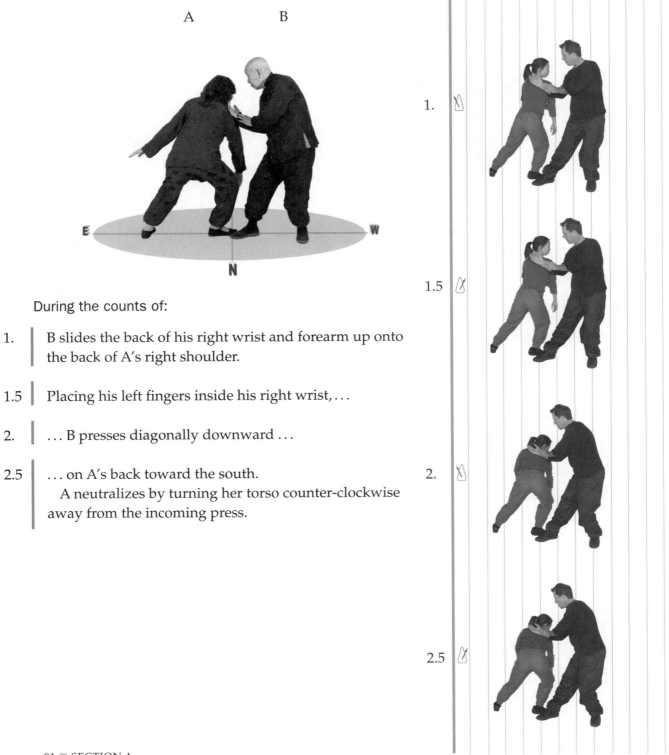

A B

E W

N

During the counts of:

1. | B slides the back of his right wrist and forearm up onto the back of A's right shoulder.

1.5 | Placing his left fingers inside his right wrist, ...

2. | ... B presses diagonally downward ...

2.5 | ... on A's back toward the south.
A neutralizes by turning her torso counter-clockwise away from the incoming press.

1.

1.5

2.

2.5

43. Join Hands

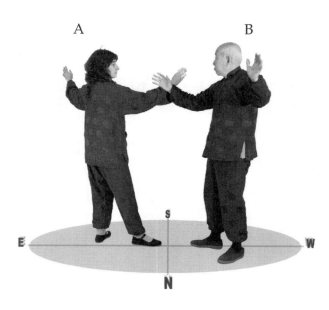

During the counts of:

1. | A, keeping her weight on her right leg,...

1.5 | ... steps back with her left foot to the south-east.

2. | Simultaneously A and B both come up ...

2.5 | ... into the "Join Hands" position.
     B is now facing south-east and A is facing north-west.

1.

1.5

2.

2.5

44. Pull / Ward Off

During the count of:

1.

B steps forward to the south-east corner with his right foot and attempts to grab A's right wrist.

A steps back with her left foot and wards off with her right hand by bringing her right arm rounded out in front of herself with her right palm facing her chest.

B's attempt to grab A's wrist having been effectively neutralized, he does not try to complete it but instead just stays attached to A's right wrist with his right hand (see detail below).

45. Split / Roll Back

During the count of:

> B steps forward to the south-east with his left foot and grasps A's right wrist with his right hand. He reaches over with his left hand and places it under A's right elbow in an attempt to "split" it by pushing down with his right hand and up with his left.

1.

> A neutralizes by stepping back with her right foot and turning her torso clockwise to her right while simultaneously attaching her left elbow to B's right elbow. She brings her right hand up over B's right wrist.*

> *This prevents B from grabbing her right wrist (see detail below).

46. Elbow Stroke

During the count of:

1.

B steps forward to the south-east with his right foot and, folding his right arm, strikes to A's chest with his right elbow. He cups his left palm over his right fist to give his striking elbow support* (see detail below).

A steps back with her left foot and protects herself by holding B's striking elbow with her left hand as she shifts her weight back onto her left leg to neutralize the incoming strike. She keeps her right hand lightly attached to B's right wrist (see detail below).

47. Push

During the count of:

1.

A shifts her weight onto her right foot and pushes B's elbow with her left hand, continuing to keep her right hand attached to his right wrist.

B neutralizes A's push by letting his right arm collapse and straighten out (see detail below) as he shifts his weight back onto his left leg.

48. Shoulder Stroke

A   B

E   W

During the counts of:

1.	B steps to the east and places his right foot near A's right foot to the north.
1.5	B then circles his left foot around so he is facing A to the south-east.
2.	Shifting his weight momentarily back onto his left leg …
2.5	… B then shifts his weight forward 70% onto his right foot and executes "shoulder stroke" to the right side of A's body. B's right arm hangs straight down with his palm facing in. His left hand lightly attaches to the inside of his right forearm for support. A, making sure to maintain contact with B, neutralizes the "shoulder stroke" by shifting her weight back onto her left leg and turning her waist counter-clockwise, slightly to the left.

1.

1.5

2.

2.5

49. Press

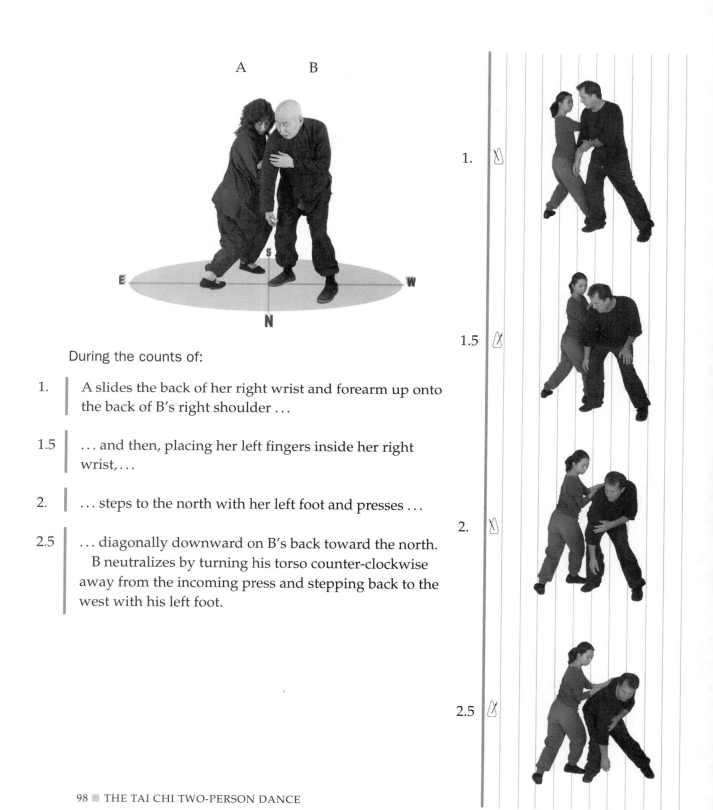

A B

During the counts of:

1. | A slides the back of her right wrist and forearm up onto the back of B's right shoulder . . .

1.5 | . . . and then, placing her left fingers inside her right wrist, . . .

2. | . . . steps to the north with her left foot and presses . . .

2.5 | . . . diagonally downward on B's back toward the north. B neutralizes by turning his torso counter-clockwise away from the incoming press and stepping back to the west with his left foot.

1.

1.5

2.

2.5

50. Join Hands

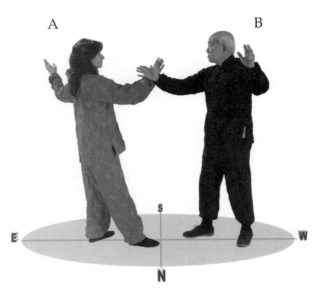

A   B

S
E   W
N

During the counts of:

1. | B neutralizes the incoming press by turning his shoulder in a counter-clockwise circular motion away from it . . .

1.5 | . . . and shifts his weight back onto his left leg.
     A shifts her weight back onto her left foot.

2. | Straightening his torso, B raises his right arm and attaches his right wrist to the back of A's right wrist.

2.5 | Both A and B now come into the "Join Hands" posture.
     A is now facing west and B is facing east.

1.

1.5

2.

2.5

Section 5

Postures 51–71

51. Step Forward and Shoulder Stroke (left style)

During the counts of:

1. | A grasps B's right wrist with her right hand and places her right foot perpendicular in front of B's right foot, toes pointing north (forming a "T").

1.5 | She then steps behind B with her left foot, toes pointing west, and controls B's right elbow by pulling it across her chest.

2. | Pause . . .

2.5 | A strikes with her left shoulder to B's right side.
B neutralizes by shifting his weight back onto his left leg and turning his waist clockwise to the right.

52. Turn Body and Push

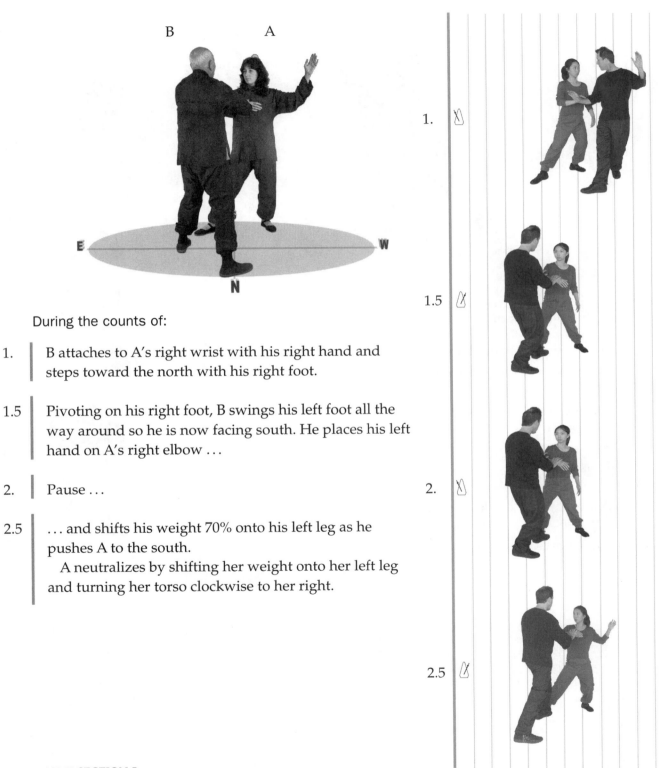

During the counts of:

1. | B attaches to A's right wrist with his right hand and steps toward the north with his right foot.

1.5 | Pivoting on his right foot, B swings his left foot all the way around so he is now facing south. He places his left hand on A's right elbow ...

2. | Pause ...

2.5 | ... and shifts his weight 70% onto his left leg as he pushes A to the south.
   A neutralizes by shifting her weight onto her left leg and turning her torso clockwise to her right.

53. Separate Hands and Kick with Sole

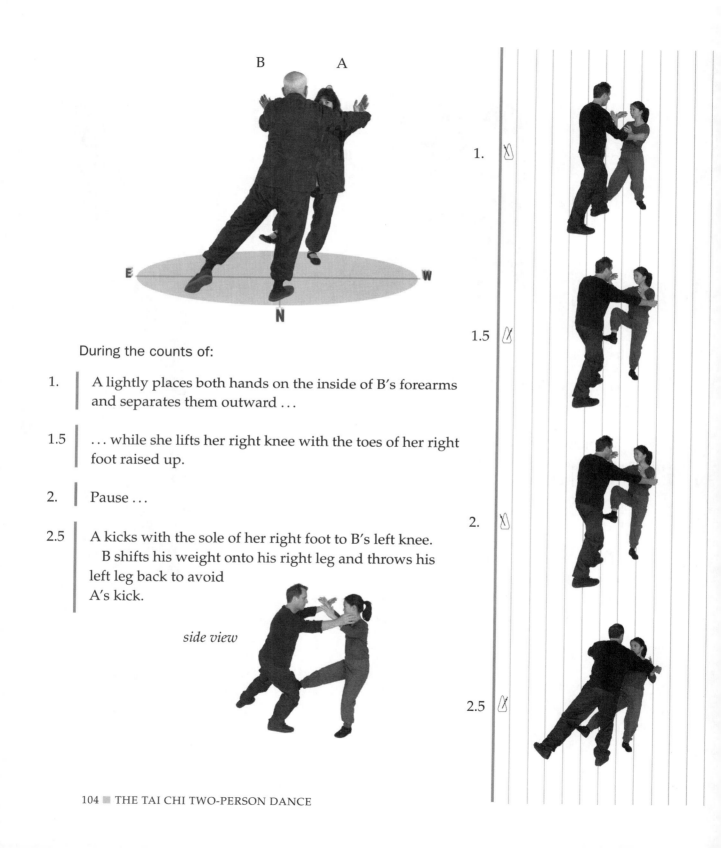

During the counts of:

1.	A lightly places both hands on the inside of B's forearms and separates them outward ...
1.5	... while she lifts her right knee with the toes of her right foot raised up.
2.	Pause ...
2.5	A kicks with the sole of her right foot to B's left knee. B shifts his weight onto his right leg and throws his left leg back to avoid A's kick.

side view

54. Punch to the Groin

During the counts of:

1. | B places his left foot down and prepares to step forward with his right foot. He lightly grasps A's right wrist with his left hand as he forms a fist with his right hand, attaching it, tiger's mouth facing out, to his right hip.
       A mirrors B's foot movement and sets her right foot down.

1.5 | B then steps toward A to the south with his right foot ...

2. | Pause ...

2.5 | ... and punches with his right fist, tiger's mouth facing up, to A's groin as he shifts his weight 70% onto his right foot.
       A momentarily shifts her weight onto her right foot and steps backward with her left foot. She intercepts B's incoming punch by clockwise circling her right wrist underneath B's right wrist and shifting her weight back onto her left foot.

55. Step Forward, Pull, and Split

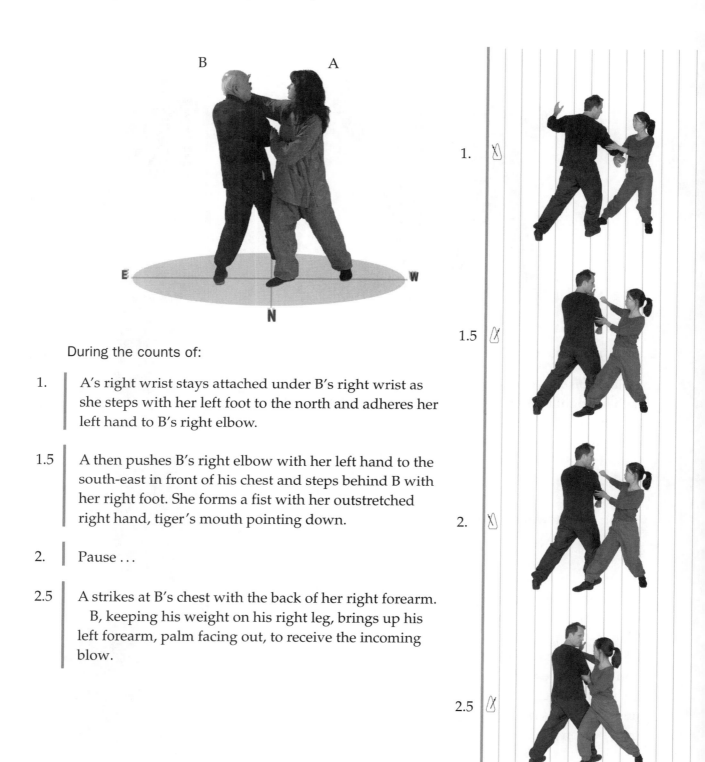

During the counts of:

1. | A's right wrist stays attached under B's right wrist as she steps with her left foot to the north and adheres her left hand to B's right elbow.

1.5 | A then pushes B's right elbow with her left hand to the south-east in front of his chest and steps behind B with her right foot. She forms a fist with her outstretched right hand, tiger's mouth pointing down.

2. | Pause . . .

2.5 | A strikes at B's chest with the back of her right forearm. B, keeping his weight on his right leg, brings up his left forearm, palm facing out, to receive the incoming blow.

56. Change Step and Fair Lady Weaving with a Shuttle

During the counts of:

1. | B steps to the north with his right foot, toes pointing to the north-west corner, while he lightly grasps A's right wrist with his right hand.

1.5 | He then steps with his left foot to the south-west, placing it slightly behind A's right foot so that his knee touches hers.

2. | B's left wrist now adheres underneath A's right elbow, and as he lifts it up, diagonally outward, he rotates his left palm out in a turning (screw) motion. His left lower leg "locks" A's right knee.

2.5 | B now strikes to underneath A's right arm with his right palm.
   A neutralizes by shifting her weight back onto her left leg and hollowing her chest.

57. Left Ward Off and Right Chop with Fist

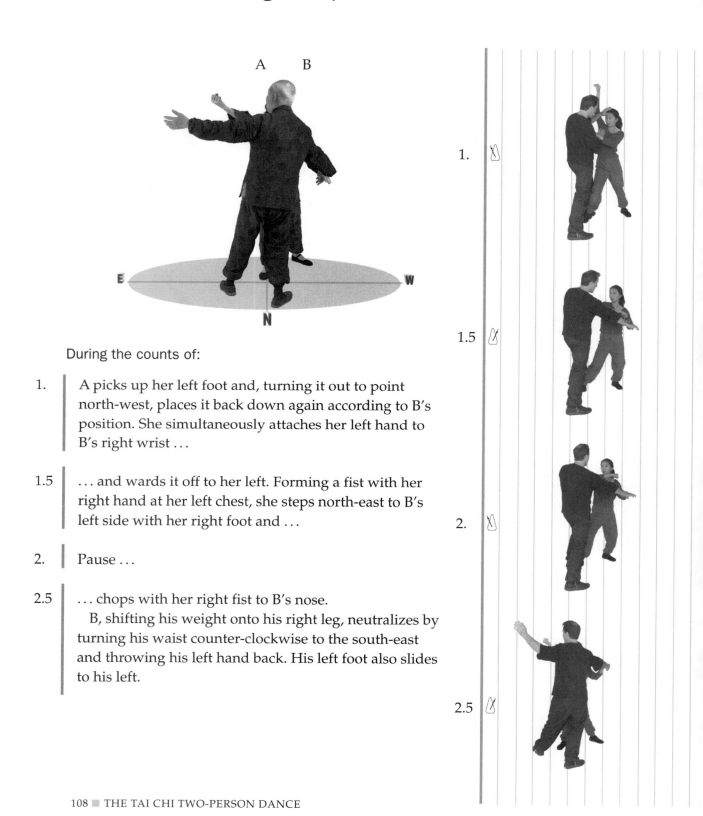

A   B

E   W

N

During the counts of:

1. | A picks up her left foot and, turning it out to point north-west, places it back down again according to B's position. She simultaneously attaches her left hand to B's right wrist . . .

1.5 | . . . and wards it off to her left. Forming a fist with her right hand at her left chest, she steps north-east to B's left side with her right foot and . . .

2. | Pause . . .

2.5 | . . . chops with her right fist to B's nose.
B, shifting his weight onto his right leg, neutralizes by turning his waist counter-clockwise to the south-east and throwing his left hand back. His left foot also slides to his left.

1.

1.5

2.

2.5

58. White Crane Spreading Wings and Kick with Left Sole

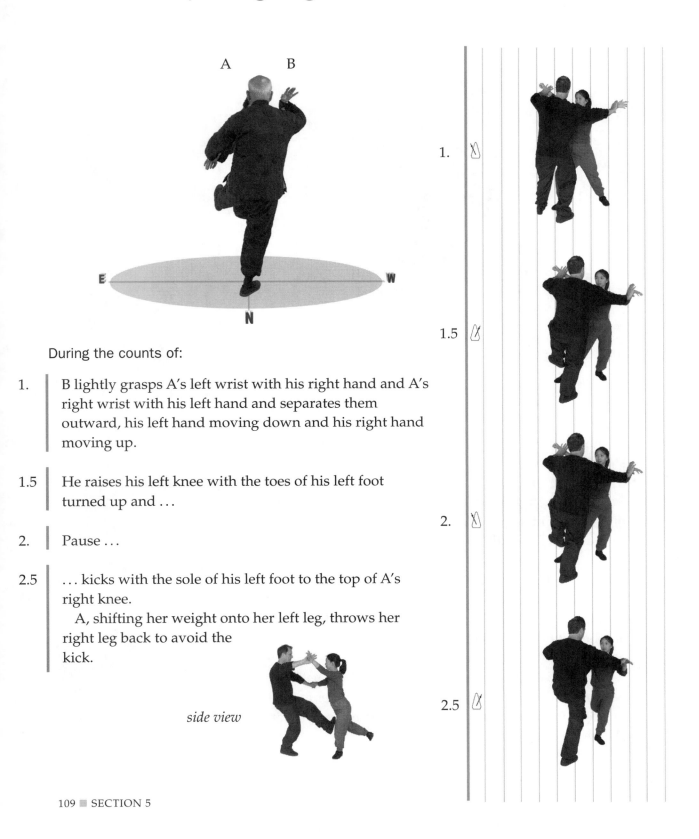

During the counts of:

1. | B lightly grasps A's left wrist with his right hand and A's right wrist with his left hand and separates them outward, his left hand moving down and his right hand moving up.

1.5 | He raises his left knee with the toes of his left foot turned up and ...

2. | Pause ...

2.5 | ... kicks with the sole of his left foot to the top of A's right knee.
A, shifting her weight onto her left leg, throws her right leg back to avoid the kick.

side view

59. Step Forward and Shoulder Stroke (left style)

During the counts of:

1.	A, with her right palm, reaches down and adheres to the inside of B's left ankle and . . .
1.5	. . . pushes it to the north-east corner while "hop" stepping in the same direction with her right foot.
2.	Shifting her weight onto the right foot, she now lets go of B's foot and turns to face B to the west. Stepping between his feet with her left foot . . .
2.5	. . . she shifts her weight 70% onto her left foot and strikes at the right side of B's body with her left side and shoulder. Her left arm is straight down, palm facing in, and her right hand is lightly touching behind her left elbow. B neutralizes the incoming strike by taking a half-step back with his left foot and shifting his weight onto it. He makes sure to maintain contact with her left forearm and elbow.

60. Step Back and Hammer A's Left Arm

A   B

During the counts of:

1. | B circles his left wrist underneath and around A's left wrist. Grasping the wrist, he shifts his weight onto his left foot ...

1.5 | ... and pivots his right toes to face north. B then shifts his weight back onto his right foot and ...

2. | ... swings his left foot around so that he is facing north in a "horse stance." As he does this he pulls A's left hand with him toward the west.

2.5 | B hammers A's upturned left elbow with his right fist. A sinks her weight down and twists her left arm counter-clockwise to neutralize B's hammer blow.

1.

1.5

2.

2.5

61. Turn Body and Roll Back

A   B

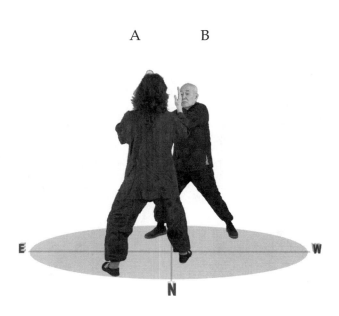

During the counts of:

1. | A takes a step with her right foot to the north-west.

1.5 | Grasping B's left wrist with her left hand, A pivots on her right toes and ...

2. | Pause ...

2.5 | ... steps with her left foot to the north-east. She uses this momentum to pull B's left wrist and arm with her to the north-east. She comes into the "roll back" position facing south-east with her right elbow attaching to B's left elbow.

    B, stepping with his right foot, allows himself to be pulled toward the north-east corner.

1.

1.5

2.

2.5

62. Strike with Two Fists

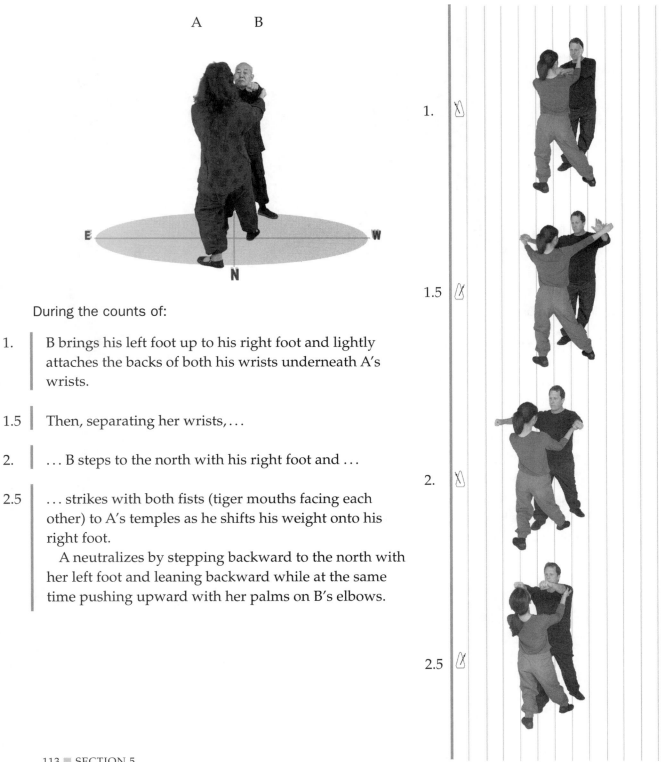

A   B

E   W

N

1.

1.5

2.

2.5

During the counts of:

1. | B brings his left foot up to his right foot and lightly attaches the backs of both his wrists underneath A's wrists.

1.5 | Then, separating her wrists, . . .

2. | . . . B steps to the north with his right foot and . . .

2.5 | . . . strikes with both fists (tiger mouths facing each other) to A's temples as he shifts his weight onto his right foot.

    A neutralizes by stepping backward to the north with her left foot and leaning backward while at the same time pushing upward with her palms on B's elbows.

63. Step Forward and Push with Two Hands

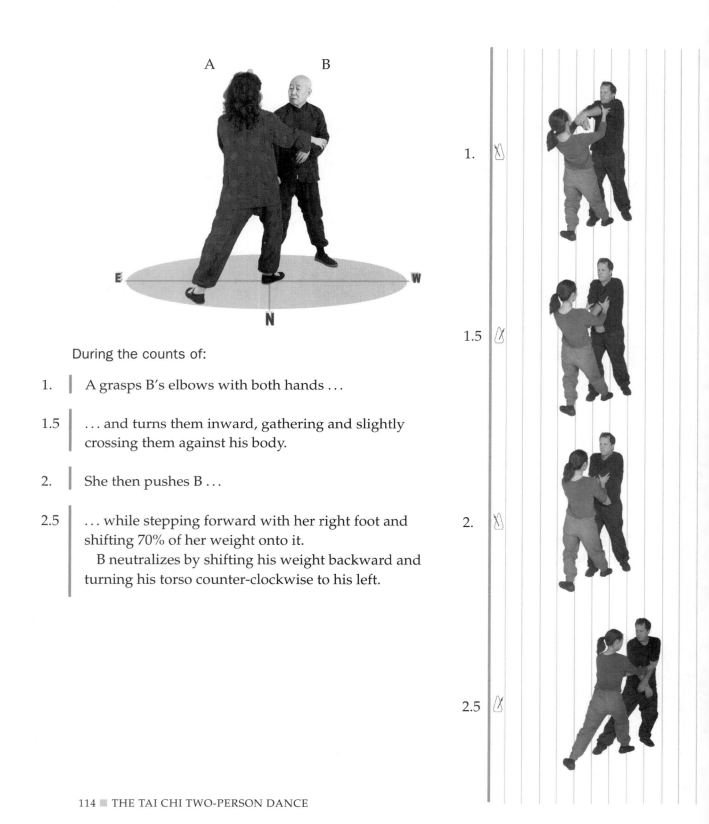

During the counts of:

1. | A grasps B's elbows with both hands . . .

1.5 | . . . and turns them inward, gathering and slightly crossing them against his body.

2. | She then pushes B . . .

2.5 | . . . while stepping forward with her right foot and shifting 70% of her weight onto it.
   B neutralizes by shifting his weight backward and turning his torso counter-clockwise to his left.

64. Squatting Down, Ward Off, and Punch

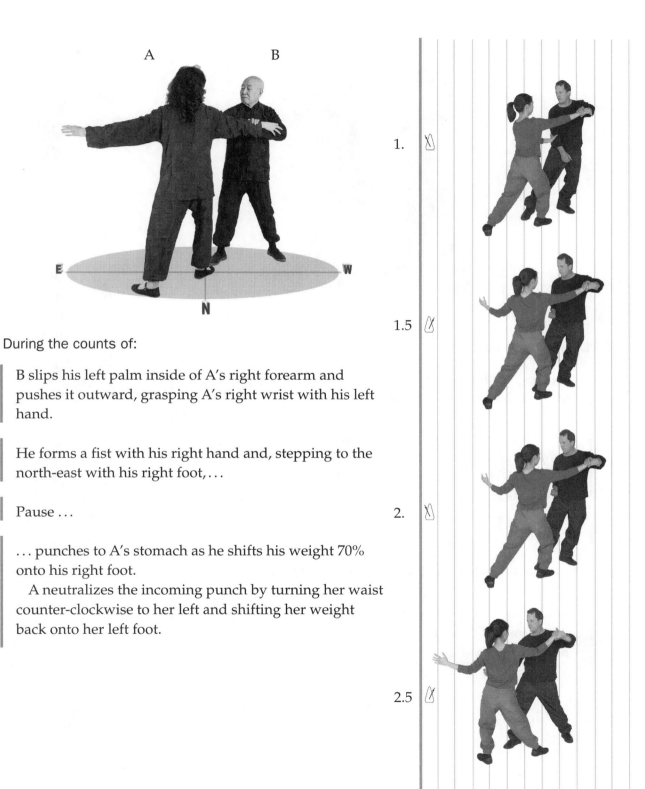

During the counts of:

1. | B slips his left palm inside of A's right forearm and pushes it outward, grasping A's right wrist with his left hand.

1.5 | He forms a fist with his right hand and, stepping to the north-east with his right foot,...

2. | Pause...

2.5 | ... punches to A's stomach as he shifts his weight 70% onto his right foot.
A neutralizes the incoming punch by turning her waist counter-clockwise to her left and shifting her weight back onto her left foot.

65. Push with Left Hand

During the counts of:

1. | A circles her right wrist around B's outstretched right fist while she steps to the east with her right foot.

1.5 | She then spins her left foot around into a "bow stance" facing south-west, with her right hand grasping B's right wrist. Her left hand adheres to B's right upper arm.
    B adjusts his left foot so as to face A to the north-east.

2. | Pause . . .

2.5 | Holding B's right arm downward against his body, A shifts her weight 70% onto her left leg and pushes with her left hand on B's right upper arm.
    B neutralizes by shifting his weight onto his left leg and turning his waist clockwise to his right.

1.

1.5

2.

2.5

66. Twist A's Right Arm

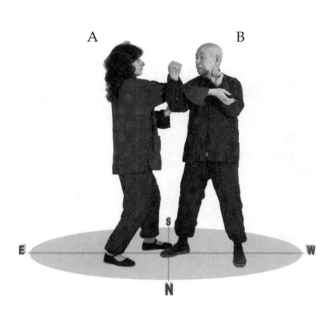

During the counts of:

1. | B steps to the north with his left foot while circling his left hand over A's right wrist.

1.5 | B attaches his left wrist to the inside of A's right wrist.

2. | Stepping east into a "bow stance," B makes a fist with his right hand and brings it up underneath to the outside of A's elbow, catching it in the belly of his right forearm.

2.5 | He then applies pressure on her right forearm by turning his waist to face A to the east.
     A twists her right arm counter-clockwise and pulls it back to avoid having her elbow "locked."

67. Take Advantage and Push

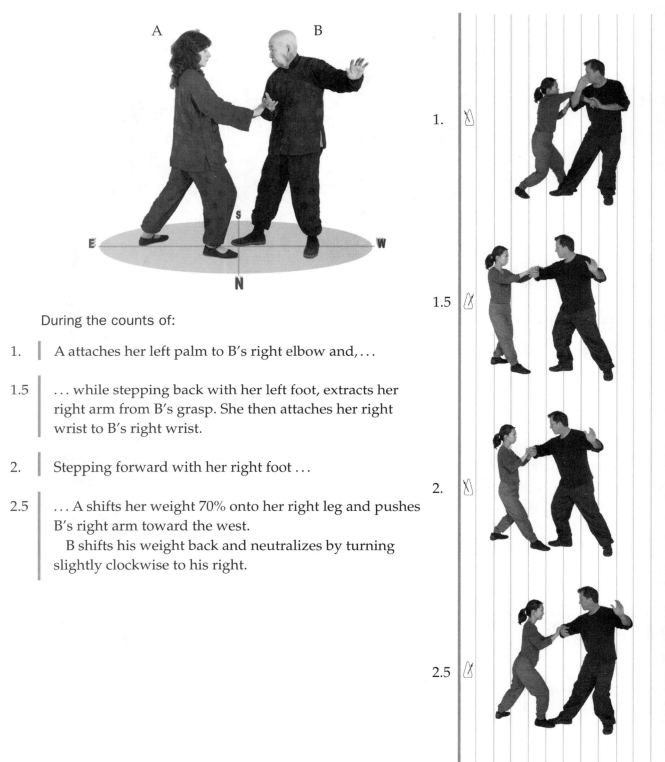

During the counts of:

1. | A attaches her left palm to B's right elbow and,...

1.5 | ... while stepping back with her left foot, extracts her right arm from B's grasp. She then attaches her right wrist to B's right wrist.

2. | Stepping forward with her right foot ...

2.5 | ... A shifts her weight 70% onto her right leg and pushes B's right arm toward the west.
   B shifts his weight back and neutralizes by turning slightly clockwise to his right.

68. Neutralize and Strike with Right Palm

During the counts of:

1. | B adheres with his wrists to the inside of A's wrists and separates both her hands outward.

1.5 | Stepping toward A with his right foot . . .

2. | . . . B shifts his weight forward and slaps with his right palm . . .

2.5 | . . . to the left side of A's head.
A avoids the slap by attaching her left palm to B's right elbow and, keeping her torso from leaning too much, squatting down to avoid the slap.

69. Neutralize and Push

During the counts of:

1. | A, keeping her left hand attached to B's left elbow, stands up and attaches her right hand to B's right wrist . . .

1.5 | . . . and steps forward to the west with her right foot.

2. | Pause . . .

2.5 | She then shifts her weight 70% forward and pushes on B's right forearm with both hands.
    B neutralizes by shifting his weight back onto his left leg.

1.

1.5

2.

2.5

70. Neutralize and Elbow Stroke

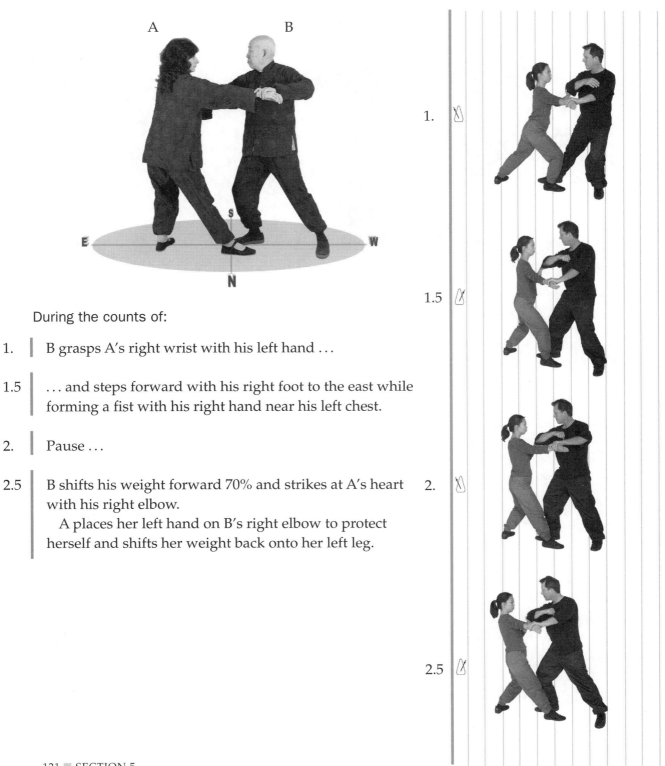

During the counts of:

1.   B grasps A's right wrist with his left hand ...

1.5   ... and steps forward with his right foot to the east while forming a fist with his right hand near his left chest.

2.   Pause ...

2.5   B shifts his weight forward 70% and strikes at A's heart with his right elbow.
      A places her left hand on B's right elbow to protect herself and shifts her weight back onto her left leg.

71. Join Hands

A   B

During the counts of:

1. | A shifts her weight 70% onto her right foot and pushes on B's right elbow with her left hand.
   | B shifts his weight back onto his left leg.

1.5 | B shifts his weight 70% forward toward A and strikes at her with his right elbow.
    | A shifts her weight back onto her left leg and maintains contact with B's striking elbow with her left hand.

2. | A pushes on B's right elbow.

2.5 | B uses the pressure on his right elbow to unfold his arm and attempts to chop at A's face with the back of his right fist.
    | A intercepts the incoming chop with the back of her right wrist.
    |
    | A and B both come up into the "Join Hands" position.

1.

1.5

2.

2.5

Section 6

Postures 72–92

Pushing Hands

72. B: Step Forward with Left Foot and Push
A: Step Back with Right Foot, Ward Off, and Roll Back

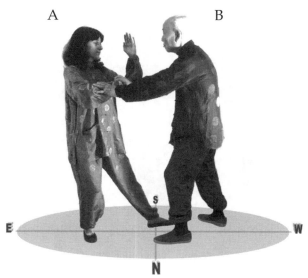

During the counts of:

1. | B steps forward with his left foot and with both hands pushes on A's right forearm as he shifts his weight 70% onto his left leg. His left fingers and palm are on her elbow, and his right palm and fingers are on her wrist. (B wants to be sure to control A's forearm. If he's not careful to place his hands on her wrist and elbow, she can slip either of these past his hands to strike him.)

    A steps back with her right foot and wards off the incoming push with her right forearm.

1.5 | A, attaching her left elbow to B's right elbow, continues to deflect B's incoming push by turning her torso to her right, performing "roll back." Her right hand turns palm up with her thumb curling over B's right wrist (see detail below).

1.

1.5

73. B: Press
A: Neutralize

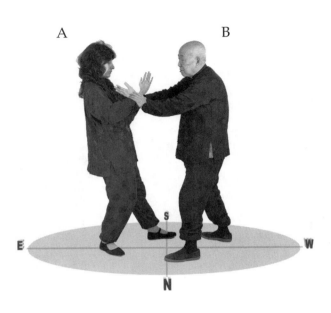

During the counts of:

1. | B's push having been neutralized, he then lightly places his left hand on his right wrist and presses diagonally to his right with the back of his right forearm to A's chest.
   A lightly attaches her left hand to the back of B's left wrist (see detail below) ...

1.5 | ... and gently guides his "press" past her, turning her torso with it counter-clockwise to her left. Her right hand remains attached to the back of B's right hand and wrist.

1.

1.5

74. A: Push
B: Ward Off and Roll Back

A   B

During the counts of:

1. | After B's "press" has passed by her chest, A slips her right hand over to attach to B's left elbow and attaches her left hand to B's left wrist. Controlling his forearm, A shifts her weight 70% onto her left leg and pushes toward B's chest to the west.

1.5 | B wards off the incoming push by withdrawing his weight onto his back right foot and turning his torso to his left ("roll back"), making sure to lightly adhere with his right elbow to A's left elbow. As B turns his torso to the left, his left hand turns palm up so that his thumb curls over A's left wrist (see detail below).

1.

1.5

75. A: Press
   B: Neutralize

A   B

S
E   W
N

During the counts of:

1.	A "presses" to B's chest with the back of her left hand and forearm. Her right fingers lightly attach to the inside of her left wrist, and her elbows remain slightly bent.
1.5	B lightly attaches his right hand to the back of A's right wrist and gently guides her "press" past him, turning his torso with it to his right. Without collapsing against his chest, B's left hand remains attached to the back of A's left hand/wrist (see detail below).

1.

1.5

76. B: Push
A: Ward Off and Roll Back

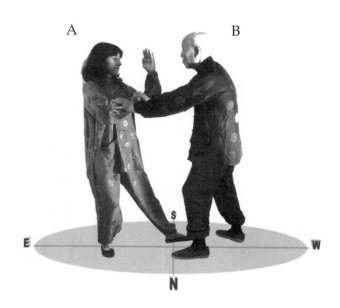

A   B

1.

1.5

During the counts of:

1.	B, with both hands, pushes on A's right forearm as he shifts his weight 70% onto his left leg. His left fingers and palm are attached to her elbow, and his right palm and fingers are on her wrist. A steps back with her right foot and wards off the incoming push with her right forearm.
1.5	Attaching her left elbow to B's right elbow, A continues to deflect the incoming push by turning her torso to her right (roll back). Her right hand turns palm up with her thumb curling over B's right wrist (see detail below).

77. B: Press
A: Neutralize

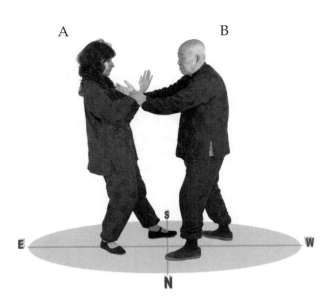

During the counts of:

1.   B's push having been neutralized, he then lightly places his left hand on his right wrist and presses diagonally to the right with the back of his right forearm to A's chest.

1.5   A lightly attaches her left hand to the back of B's left wrist and gently guides his "press" past her, turning her torso with it to her left.

78. A: Circle Hands
B: Circle Hands

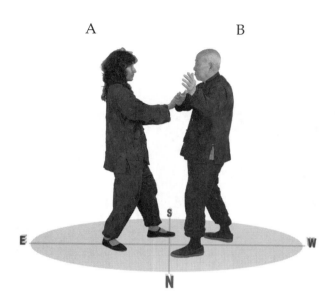

During the counts of:

1.   After B's "press" has passed by her chest, A attaches her left hand to B's left wrist and her right hand to B's left elbow. Controlling his left forearm, she circles it counter-clockwise by pushing it down and up one full turn before throwing it off to her right in an attempt to create a space or opening to push on B's chest.

1.5   To defend against the possibility of A's push, B quickly brings up his right forearm to intercept and attach to A's hands.

1.

1.5

79. A: Step Forward with Right Foot and Push
B: Step Back with Left Foot, Ward Off, and Roll Back

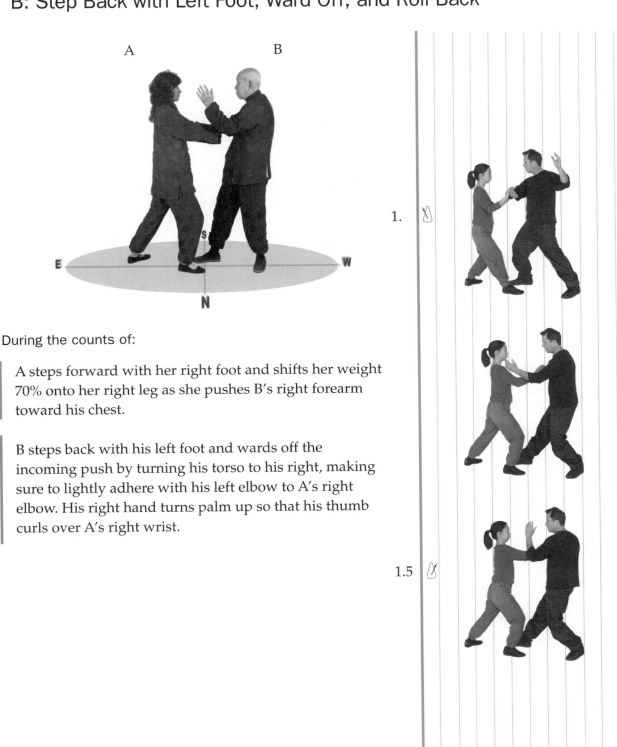

During the counts of:

1. | A steps forward with her right foot and shifts her weight 70% onto her right leg as she pushes B's right forearm toward his chest.

1.5 | B steps back with his left foot and wards off the incoming push by turning his torso to his right, making sure to lightly adhere with his left elbow to A's right elbow. His right hand turns palm up so that his thumb curls over A's right wrist.

80. A: Press
B: Neutralize

During the counts of:

1. | A "presses" to B's chest with her right hand and forearm. Her left fingers lightly attach to the inside of her right wrist.

1.5 | B lightly attaches his left hand to the back of A's left wrist and gently guides her "press" past him, turning his torso counter-clockwise to his left.

1.

1.5

81. B: Push
A: Ward Off and Roll Back

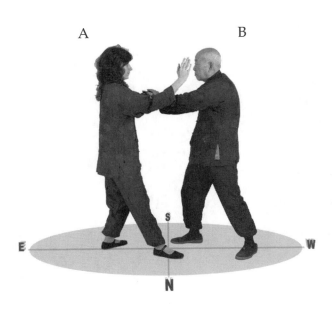

During the counts of:

1. After A's "press" has passed by his chest, B attaches his right hand to A's left elbow and his left hand to A's left wrist. Controlling her forearm, B pushes it toward A's chest as he shifts his weight 70% onto his right leg.

1.5 A withdraws her weight back onto her left foot and wards off the incoming push with her left forearm. Attaching her right elbow to B's left elbow, she continues to deflect the incoming push by turning her torso to her left, performing the "roll back" posture. Her left hand turns palm up with her thumb curling over B's left wrist.

1.

1.5

82. B: Press
A: Neutralize

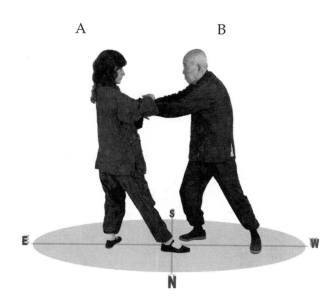

During the counts of:

1. | B's push having been neutralized, he then lightly places his right hand on his left wrist and presses diagonally to the north-east with the back of his left forearm to A's chest.

1.5 | A lightly attaches her right hand to the back of B's right wrist and gently guides his "press" past her as she neutralizes it by turning her torso to her right.

83. A: Push
B: Ward Off and Roll Back

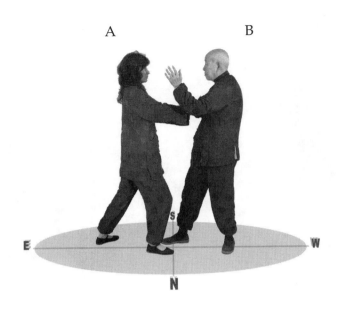

A   B

E   S   W   N

1.

1.5

During the counts of:

1.	After B's "press" has passed by her chest, A attaches her right hand to B's right wrist and her left hand to B's right elbow. Controlling his forearm, A pushes it toward B's chest as she shifts her weight 70% onto her right leg.
1.5	B wards off the incoming push by turning his torso to his right, making sure to lightly adhere with his left elbow to A's right elbow. His right hand turns palm up so that his thumb curls over A's right wrist.

84. A: Press
B: Neutralize

During the counts of:

1. | A presses to B's chest with her right hand and forearm. Her left fingers lightly attach to the inside of her right wrist.

1.5 | B lightly attaches his left hand to the back of A's left wrist and gently guides her "press" past him, turning his torso to his left.

1.

1.5

85. B: Push
A: Ward Off and Roll Back

During the counts of:

1. | After A's "press" has passed by his chest, B attaches his right hand to A's left elbow and his left hand to A's left wrist. Controlling her forearm, B pushes it toward A's chest as he shifts his weight 70% onto his right leg.

1.5 | A withdraws her weight back onto her left foot and wards off the incoming push with her left forearm. Attaching her right elbow to B's left elbow, she continues to deflect the incoming push by turning her torso to her left (roll back). Her left hand turns palm up with her thumb curling over B's left wrist.

1.

1.5

86. B: Press
A: Neutralize

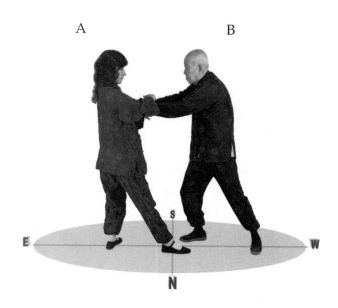

A   B

During the counts of:

1. | B's push having been neutralized, he then lightly places his right hand on his left wrist and presses diagonally to the left with the back of his left forearm to A's chest.

1.5 | A lightly attaches her right hand to the back of B's right wrist and gently guides his "press" past her as she neutralizes it by turning her torso to her right.

1.

1.5

87. A: Hands Circling Counter-clockwise and Step Forward with Left Foot
B: Hands Circling Clockwise and Step Back with Right Foot

During the counts of:

1. After B's "press" has passed by her chest, A attaches her left hand to B's right elbow and her right hand to B's right wrist. Controlling his forearm, A circles it counter-clockwise while simultaneously stepping forward with her left foot.

1.5 B follows A's circular movement with his right forearm and mirrors A's step by stepping back with his right foot. He simultaneously brings his left hand up to attach to A's right elbow.

   A brings her left hand up and attaches her fingers to her right wrist to "press."

1.

1.5

88. A: Hands Circling Counter-clockwise and Step Forward with Right Foot
B: Hands Circling Clockwise and Step Back with Left Foot

1.

1.5

During the counts of:

1. | B continues to circle A's forearm clockwise and steps backward with his left foot.

1.5 | A follows the circling movement and mirrors B's step by stepping forward with her right foot. Her left hand attaches to B's left wrist, and her right hand attaches to B's left elbow.

B brings his right hand up and attaches his fingers to the back of his left wrist to press.

89. A: Hands Circling Counter-clockwise and Step Forward with Left Foot
B: Hands Circling Clockwise and Step Back with Right Foot

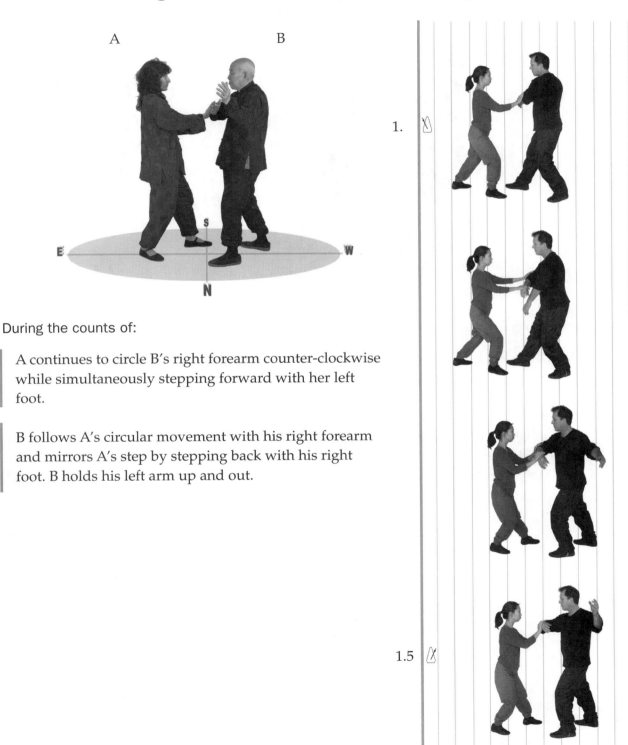

During the counts of:

1.   A continues to circle B's right forearm counter-clockwise while simultaneously stepping forward with her left foot.

1.5 B follows A's circular movement with his right forearm and mirrors A's step by stepping back with his right foot. B holds his left arm up and out.

90. A: Hands Circling Clockwise and Step Forward with Right Foot
B: Hands Circling Counter-clockwise and Step Back with Left Foot

1.

During the counts of:

1. | A now circles B's forearm clockwise and steps forward with her right foot.

1.5 | B follows the circling movement and mirrors A's step by stepping back with his left foot. He brings his left hand up and attaches his left fingers to the back of his right wrist to "press" (see detail below).

1.5

91. A: Hands Circling Clockwise and Step Forward with Left Foot
B: Hands Circling Counter-clockwise and Step Back with Right Foot

During the counts of:

1.	A circles B's right forearm clockwise while simultaneously stepping forward with her left foot.
1.5	B follows A's circular movement with his right forearm and mirrors A's step by stepping back with his right foot. He simultaneously brings his right hand up to attach to A's right elbow. A brings her right hand up and attaches her fingers to her right wrist to "press."

92. A: Hands Circling Clockwise and Step Forward with Right Foot
B: Hands Circling Counter-clockwise and Step Back with Left Foot

During the counts of:

1.	B continues to circle A's right forearm counter-clockwise and steps backward with his left foot.
1.5	A follows the circling movement and mirrors B's step by stepping forward with her right foot. Her right hand attaches to B's right wrist, and her left hand attaches to B's right elbow. B brings his left arm up and holds his left hand open out to his left.

Section 7

Postures 93–109

93. Step Forward and Horizontal Split (right style)

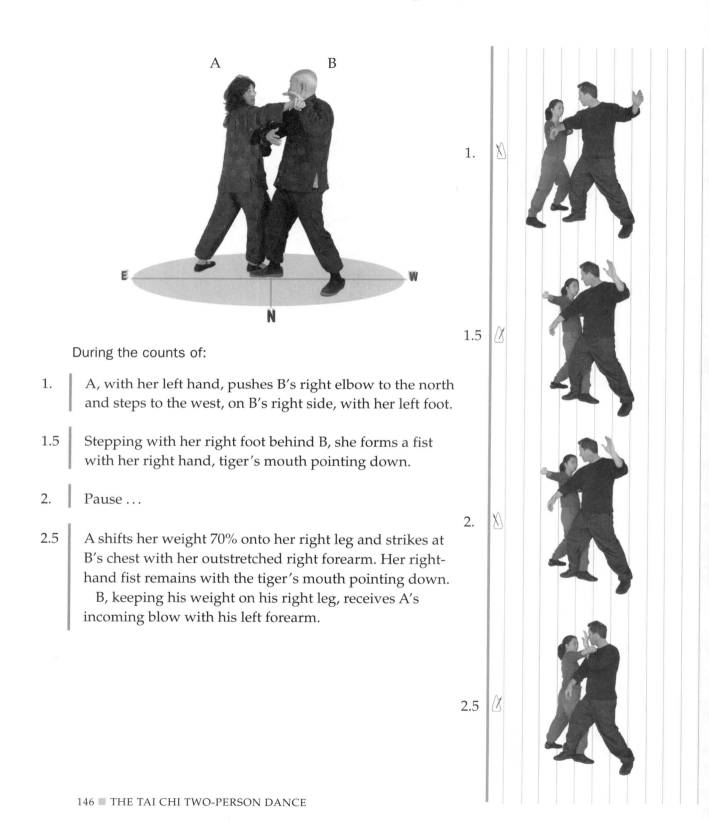

During the counts of:

1.	A, with her left hand, pushes B's right elbow to the north and steps to the west, on B's right side, with her left foot.
1.5	Stepping with her right foot behind B, she forms a fist with her right hand, tiger's mouth pointing down.
2.	Pause ...
2.5	A shifts her weight 70% onto her right leg and strikes at B's chest with her outstretched right forearm. Her right-hand fist remains with the tiger's mouth pointing down. B, keeping his weight on his right leg, receives A's incoming blow with his left forearm.

94. Change Step and Hammer A's Right Arm

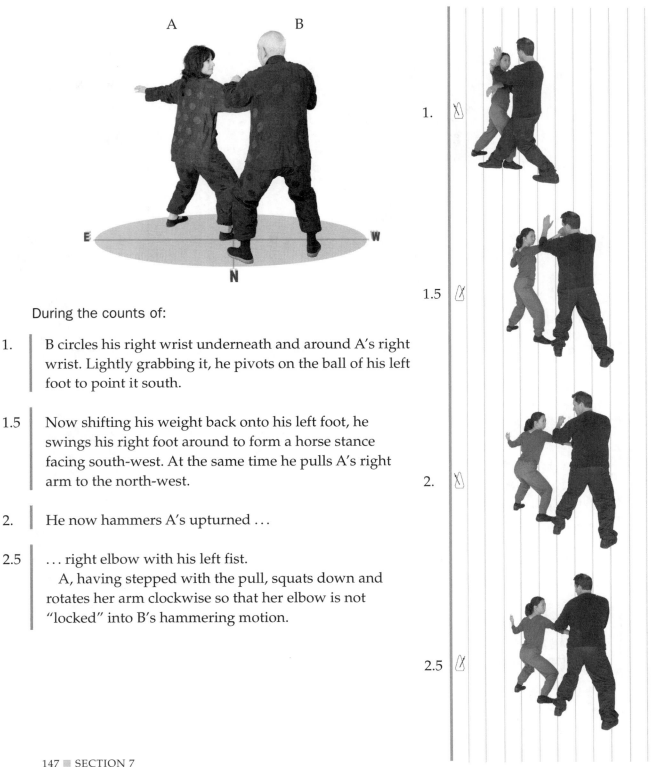

During the counts of:

1. | B circles his right wrist underneath and around A's right wrist. Lightly grabbing it, he pivots on the ball of his left foot to point it south.

1.5 | Now shifting his weight back onto his left foot, he swings his right foot around to form a horse stance facing south-west. At the same time he pulls A's right arm to the north-west.

2. | He now hammers A's upturned . . .

2.5 | . . . right elbow with his left fist.
A, having stepped with the pull, squats down and rotates her arm clockwise so that her elbow is not "locked" into B's hammering motion.

95. Strike Tiger (right style)

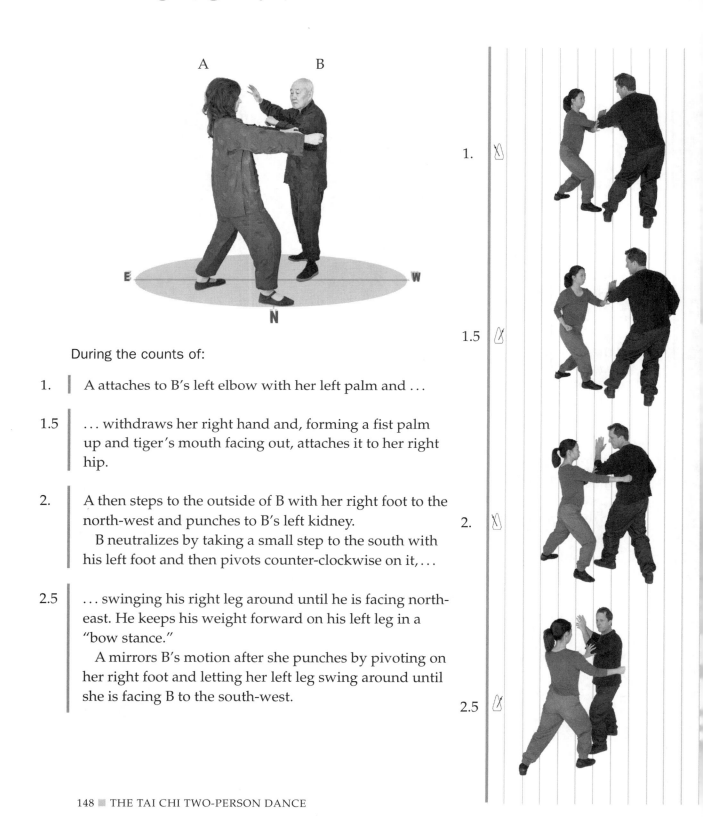

A   B

E   W

N

During the counts of:

1. | A attaches to B's left elbow with her left palm and ...

1.5 | ... withdraws her right hand and, forming a fist palm up and tiger's mouth facing out, attaches it to her right hip.

2. | A then steps to the outside of B with her right foot to the north-west and punches to B's left kidney.
B neutralizes by taking a small step to the south with his left foot and then pivots counter-clockwise on it, ...

2.5 | ... swinging his right leg around until he is facing northeast. He keeps his weight forward on his left leg in a "bow stance."
A mirrors B's motion after she punches by pivoting on her right foot and letting her left leg swing around until she is facing B to the south-west.

1.

1.5

2.

2.5

96. Turn Body, Withdraw Step, and Roll Back

During the counts of:

1. | B places the ball of his right foot near A's left foot and grasps A's left wrist with his left hand.

1.5 | He then pivots on the ball of his right foot and swings his left foot around, ending up in a "horse stance" with his feet facing south-west.

2. | Pause . . .

2.5 | B attaches his right elbow to A's left elbow and, turning his torso counter-clockwise to face southwest, applies "roll back."
  A neutralizes by sitting down and slightly rotating her arm counter-clockwise so that her elbow joint cannot be "locked" into B's roll back motion.

97. Step Forward and Shoulder Stroke

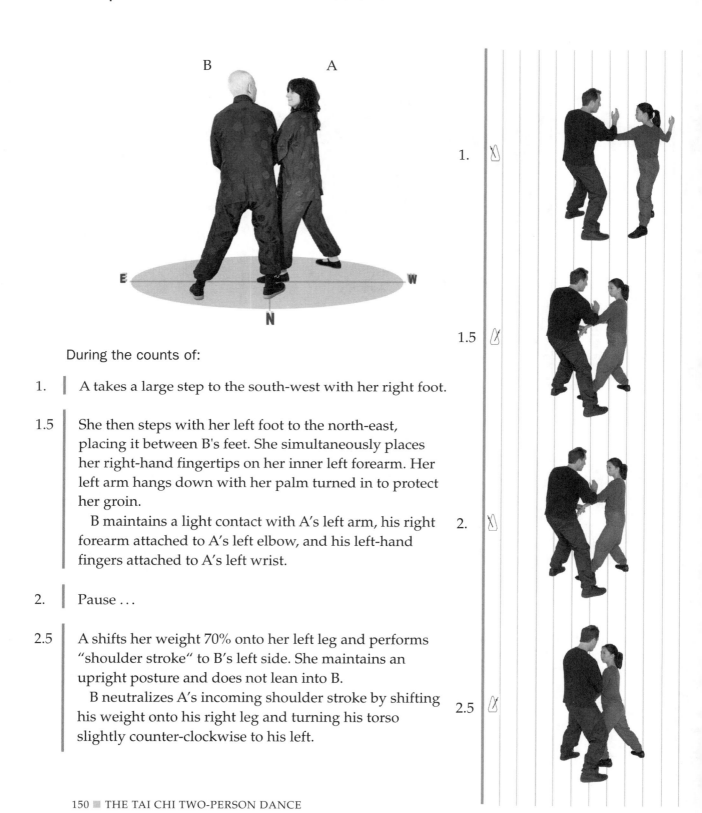

B   A

E   W

N

During the counts of:

1. | A takes a large step to the south-west with her right foot.

1.5 | She then steps with her left foot to the north-east, placing it between B's feet. She simultaneously places her right-hand fingertips on her inner left forearm. Her left arm hangs down with her palm turned in to protect her groin.
    B maintains a light contact with A's left arm, his right forearm attached to A's left elbow, and his left-hand fingers attached to A's left wrist.

2. | Pause . . .

2.5 | A shifts her weight 70% onto her left leg and performs "shoulder stroke" to B's left side. She maintains an upright posture and does not lean into B.
    B neutralizes A's incoming shoulder stroke by shifting his weight onto his right leg and turning his torso slightly counter-clockwise to his left.

1.

1.5

2.

2.5

98. Press

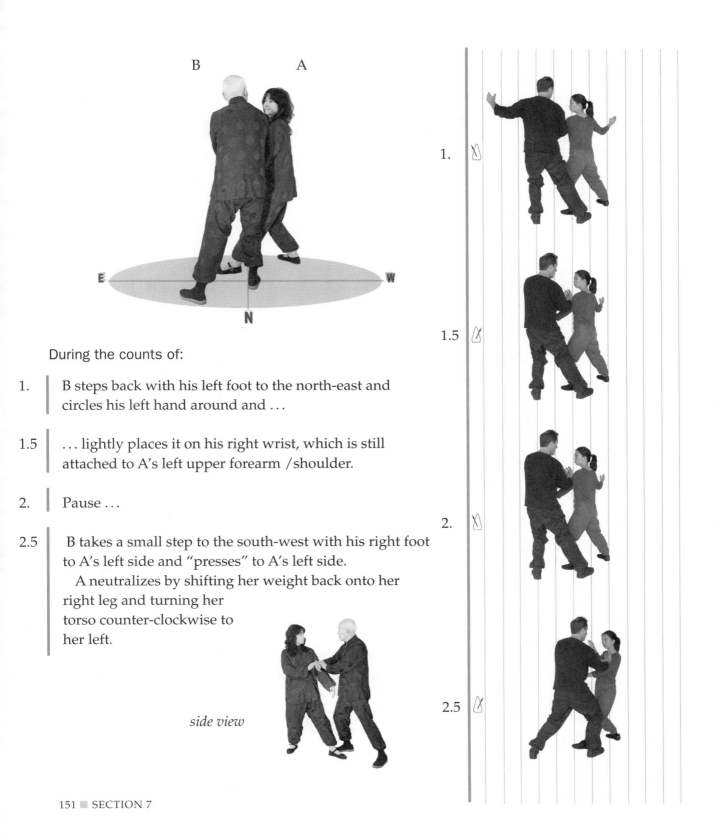

During the counts of:

1. | B steps back with his left foot to the north-east and circles his left hand around and …

1.5 | … lightly places it on his right wrist, which is still attached to A's left upper forearm /shoulder.

2. | Pause …

2.5 | B takes a small step to the south-west with his right foot to A's left side and "presses" to A's left side.
A neutralizes by shifting her weight back onto her right leg and turning her torso counter-clockwise to her left.

side view

99. Change Step, Separate Both Hands, and Shoulder Stroke

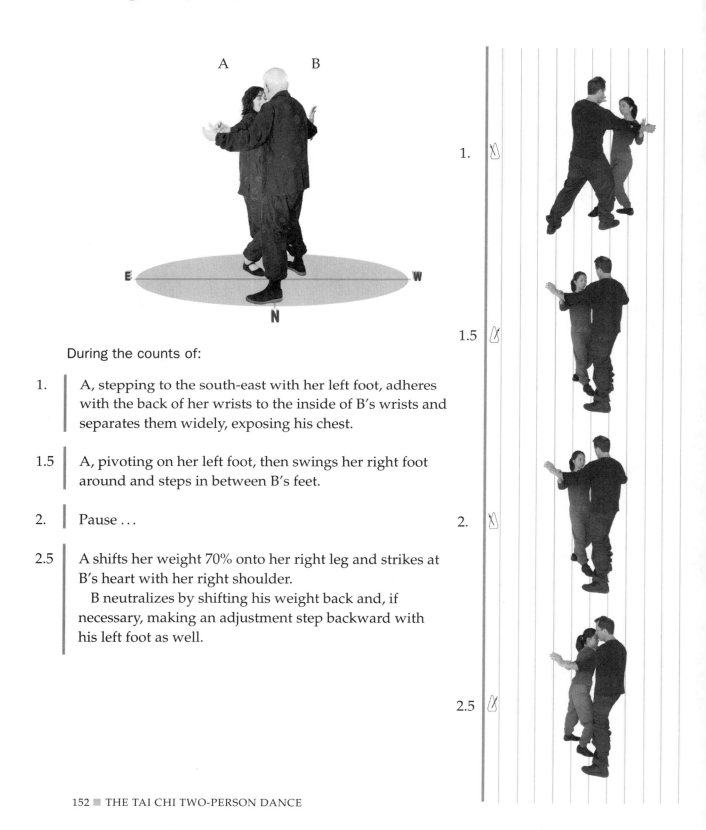

During the counts of:

1. | A, stepping to the south-east with her left foot, adheres with the back of her wrists to the inside of B's wrists and separates them widely, exposing his chest.

1.5 | A, pivoting on her left foot, then swings her right foot around and steps in between B's feet.

2. | Pause . . .

2.5 | A shifts her weight 70% onto her right leg and strikes at B's heart with her right shoulder.
    B neutralizes by shifting his weight back and, if necessary, making an adjustment step backward with his left foot as well.

100. Change Step, Turn Body, and Shoulder Stroke

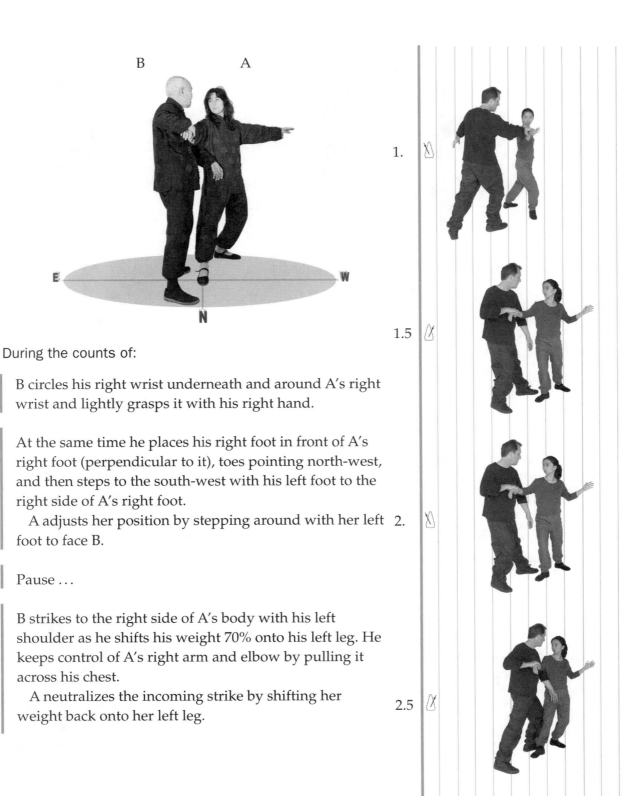

B   A

E   W

N

1.

1.5

2.

2.5

During the counts of:

1.	B circles his right wrist underneath and around A's right wrist and lightly grasps it with his right hand.
1.5	At the same time he places his right foot in front of A's right foot (perpendicular to it), toes pointing north-west, and then steps to the south-west with his left foot to the right side of A's right foot. A adjusts her position by stepping around with her left foot to face B.
2.	Pause ...
2.5	B strikes to the right side of A's body with his left shoulder as he shifts his weight 70% onto his left leg. He keeps control of A's right arm and elbow by pulling it across his chest. A neutralizes the incoming strike by shifting her weight back onto her left leg.

101. Striking Elbow (right style)

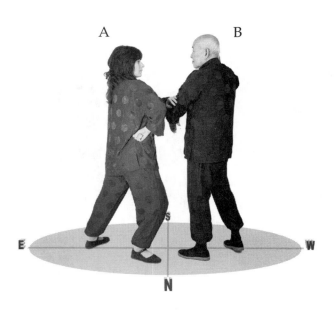

A   B

1.

1.5

2.

2.5

During the counts of:

1.	A attaches her left palm to B's left elbow.
1.5	She withdraws her right foot and forms a fist at her right hip with her right hand. She then steps with her right foot to B's left side, toes pointing north-east.
2.	Pause . . .

2.5	A shifts her weight 70% onto her right leg and with the turning motion of her torso strikes at B's left kidney with her extended right elbow.
	
	  B neutralizes the strike by taking a small step to the west with his left foot and then pivots counter-clockwise on it away from the strike, swinging his right leg around until he is facing east.
	
	  A mirrors B's neutralizing motion by pivoting on her right foot and swinging her left leg around until she is facing west.

102. B: Turn Body and Golden Rooster Stands on One Leg
A: Step Back and Neutralize

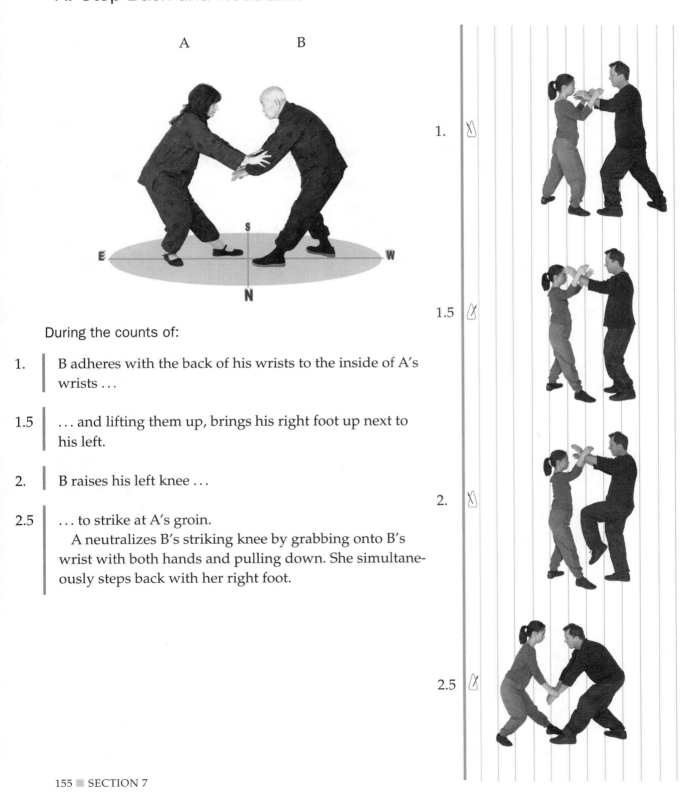

A   B

During the counts of:

1. | B adheres with the back of his wrists to the inside of A's wrists . . .

1.5 | . . . and lifting them up, brings his right foot up next to his left.

2. | B raises his left knee . . .

2.5 | . . . to strike at A's groin.
A neutralizes B's striking knee by grabbing onto B's wrist with both hands and pulling down. She simultaneously steps back with her right foot.

1.

1.5

2.

2.5

103. B: Separate Both Hands, Step Forward, and Kick with Sole
A: Step Back and Neutralize

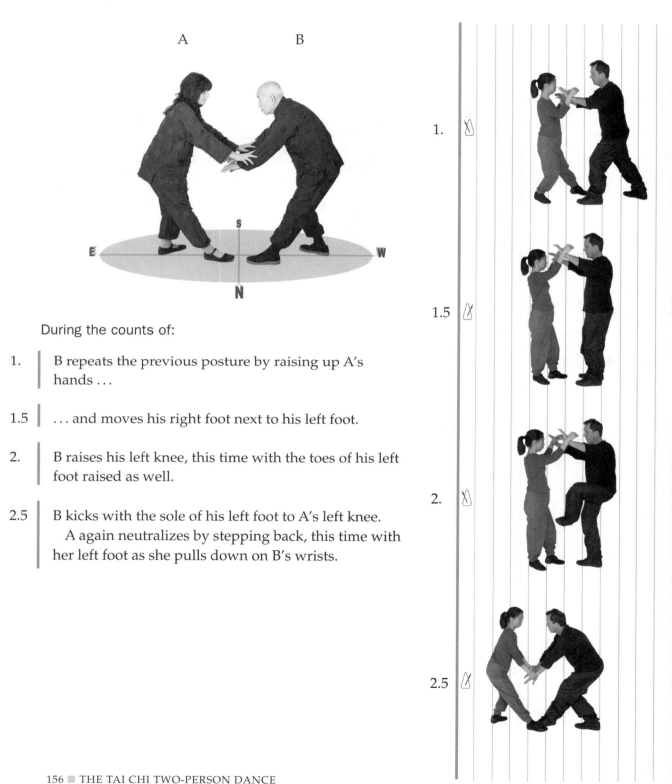

A   B

During the counts of:

1. | B repeats the previous posture by raising up A's hands . . .

1.5 | . . . and moves his right foot next to his left foot.

2. | B raises his left knee, this time with the toes of his left foot raised as well.

2.5 | B kicks with the sole of his left foot to A's left knee.
    A again neutralizes by stepping back, this time with her left foot as she pulls down on B's wrists.

1.

1.5

2.

2.5

104. Turn Body, Step Forward, and Shoulder Stroke (left style)

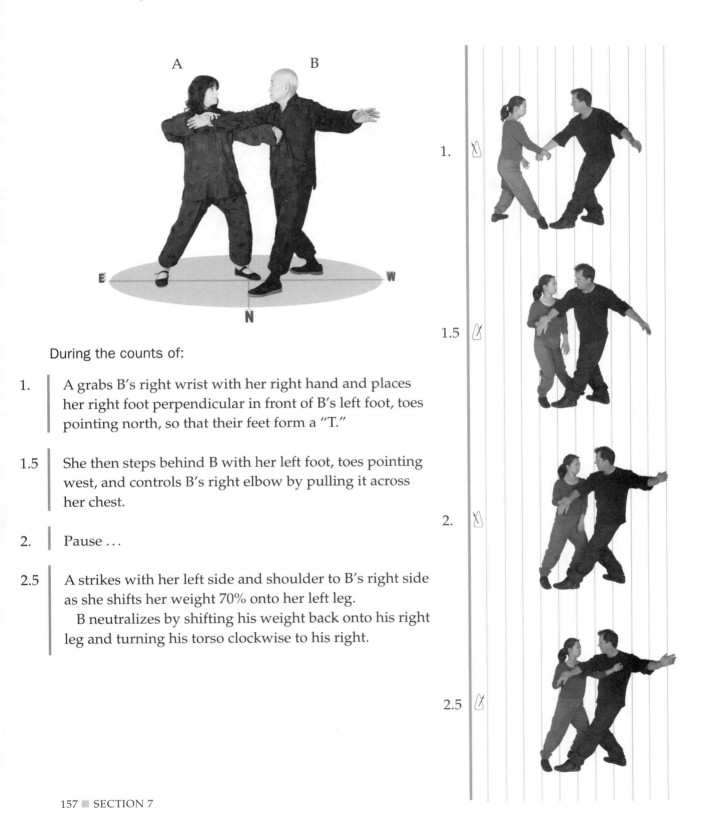

During the counts of:

1.	A grabs B's right wrist with her right hand and places her right foot perpendicular in front of B's left foot, toes pointing north, so that their feet form a "T."
1.5	She then steps behind B with her left foot, toes pointing west, and controls B's right elbow by pulling it across her chest.
2.	Pause ...
2.5	A strikes with her left side and shoulder to B's right side as she shifts her weight 70% onto her left leg. B neutralizes by shifting his weight back onto his right leg and turning his torso clockwise to his right.

105. Step Back and Hammer A's Arm

During the counts of:

1. | B circles his left wrist underneath and around A's left wrist and lightly grasps it as he shifts his weight onto his right foot.

1.5 | Pivoting on his right foot, B then swings his left foot around so that he is facing north in a horse stance. As he does this he pulls A's left hand with him and forms a fist with his right hand.

2. | B raises his right hand and . . .

2.5 | . . . hammers A's upturned left elbow with his right fist. A squats down and twists her left arm counter-clockwise to neutralize the blow.

1.

1.5

2.

2.5

106. A: Turn Body, Change Step, and Separate Foot (right style)
B: Separate Both Hands and Brush the Knee (right style)

During the counts of:

1. | A picks up her left foot and places it down so that her toes are pointing south and ...

1.5 | ... brings her right hand up to adhere to B's right wrist.

2. | Extracting her left arm from B's grasp, A lightly grasps B's right wrist with her right hand and, shifting her weight onto her left leg, ...

2.5 | ... A pulls B's right wrist to the north and kicks with her right toes to B's right knee.
   B quickly separates A's grasp on his right wrist with his left hand and steps with his right foot to the northeast to avoid A's kick. His right hand intercepts A's kick and grasps onto her right ankle from underneath.

1.

1.5

2.

2.5

107. A: Turn Body, Change Step, and Separate Foot (left style)
B: Separate Both Hands and Brush the Knee (left style)

1.

1.5

2.

2.5

During the counts of:

1. | A, in order to escape B's grasp on her right ankle, kicks upward with her right foot and …

1.5 | … places it down with toes pointing north. She lightly grasps B's left wrist with her left hand.

2. | Shifting her weight onto her right foot as she pulls B's left wrist to the south with her left hand, A kicks …

2.5 | … to B's right knee with her left toes.
  B separates A's grasp on his left wrist with his right hand and steps with his right leg to the south-east to avoid the kick. He intercepts A's left foot with his left hand and grabs onto the inside of A's left ankle (see detail below).

108. Change Hands and Shoulder Stroke

During the counts of:

1. | A, in order to escape from B's grasp on her left ankle, kicks upward with her left foot and . . .

1.5 | . . . then steps back and to the south with toes pointing south. Circling under B's right wrist with her right hand, she...

2. | . . . grasps his right wrist and, pulling it downward, steps behind B with her right foot, toes pointing west, and . . .

2.5 | . . . shifting her weight 70% onto her right leg, strikes to B's right side with her right shoulder.
   B neutralizes by shifting his weight back onto his left leg.

109. Return Shoulder Stroke

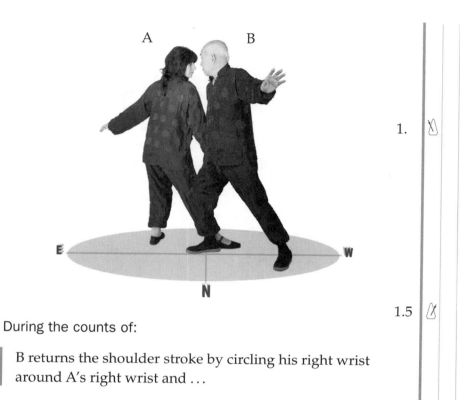

During the counts of:

1. | B returns the shoulder stroke by circling his right wrist around A's right wrist and . . .

1.5 | . . . grasping it, pulls it downward.

2. | Pause . . .

2.5 | B then steps behind A with his right foot, toes pointing east, and strikes at her right side with his right shoulder as he shift his weight 70% onto his right leg.
   A neutralizes by shifting her weight back onto her left leg.

1.

1.5

2.

2.5

Section 8

Postures 110–135

110. Step Forward and Grasp Sparrow's Tail (left style)

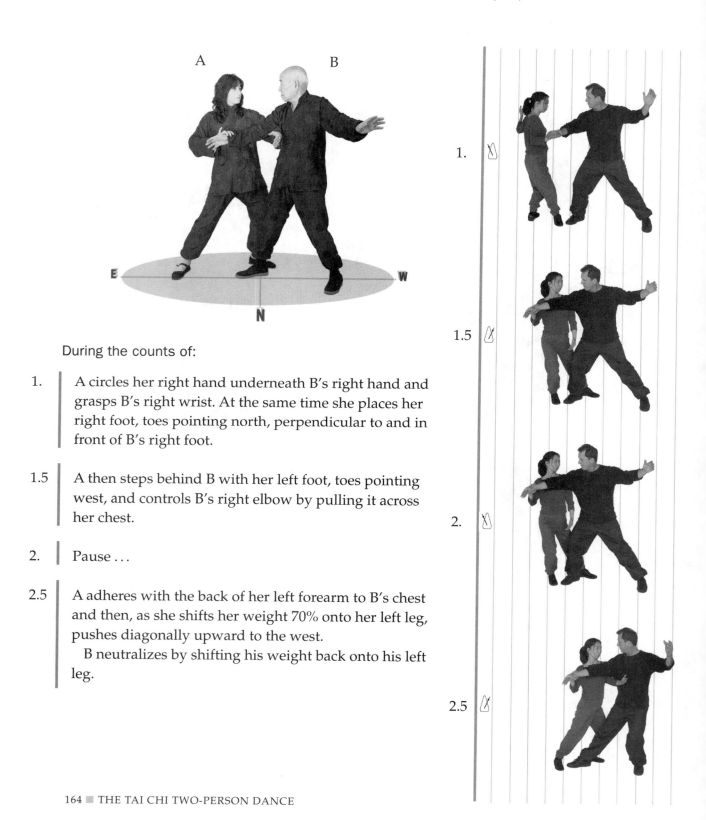

During the counts of:

1. | A circles her right hand underneath B's right hand and grasps B's right wrist. At the same time she places her right foot, toes pointing north, perpendicular to and in front of B's right foot.

1.5 | A then steps behind B with her left foot, toes pointing west, and controls B's right elbow by pulling it across her chest.

2. | Pause . . .

2.5 | A adheres with the back of her left forearm to B's chest and then, as she shifts her weight 70% onto her left leg, pushes diagonally upward to the west.
   B neutralizes by shifting his weight back onto his left leg.

111. Waving Hands in Clouds (right style)

During the counts of:

1. | B lightly grasps A's right wrist with his right hand and steps with his right foot to the north-east.

1.5 | Then, pivoting on his right foot, he swings his left leg around to rest in a "bow" stance facing south-west.

2. | Pause . . .

2.5 | He then pulls down on A's right wrist, holding her right arm against her body as he shifts his weight 70% onto his right leg, and pushes her right upper arm with his left hand.
   A neutralizes by shifting her weight back onto her left leg and turning her waist clockwise to her right. She also shifts her right foot back about one foot south to her right.

112. Step Forward and Grasp Sparrow's Tail (right style)

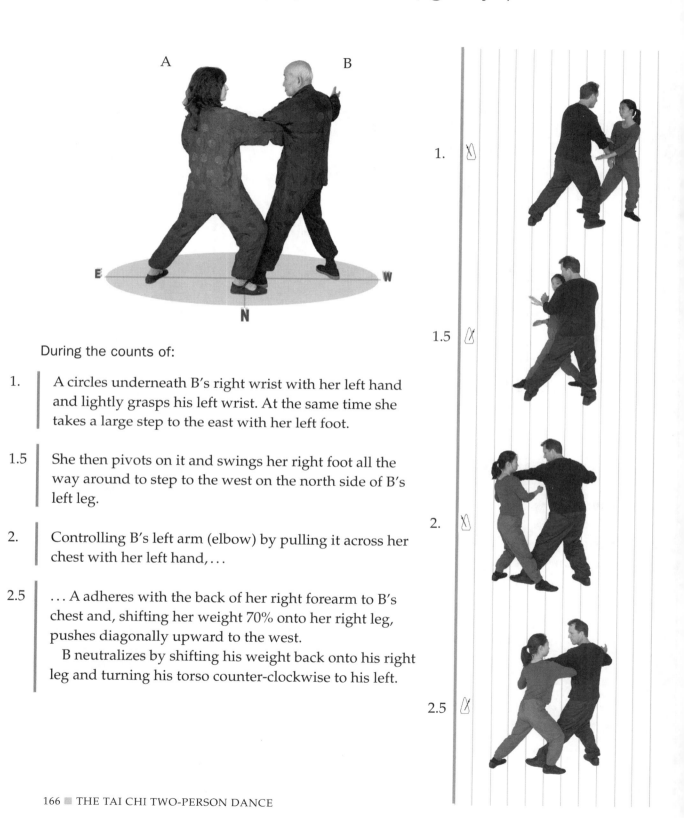

During the counts of:

1.	A circles underneath B's right wrist with her left hand and lightly grasps his left wrist. At the same time she takes a large step to the east with her left foot.
1.5	She then pivots on it and swings her right foot all the way around to step to the west on the north side of B's left leg.
2.	Controlling B's left arm (elbow) by pulling it across her chest with her left hand, . . .
2.5	. . . A adheres with the back of her right forearm to B's chest and, shifting her weight 70% onto her right leg, pushes diagonally upward to the west. B neutralizes by shifting his weight back onto his right leg and turning his torso counter-clockwise to his left.

113. Waving Hands in Clouds (left style)

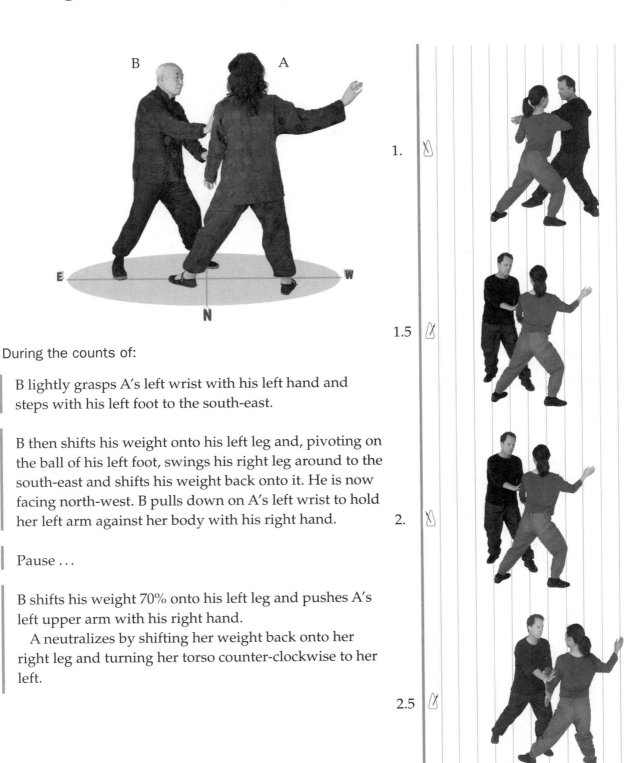

During the counts of:

1. | B lightly grasps A's left wrist with his left hand and steps with his left foot to the south-east.

1.5 | B then shifts his weight onto his left leg and, pivoting on the ball of his left foot, swings his right leg around to the south-east and shifts his weight back onto it. He is now facing north-west. B pulls down on A's left wrist to hold her left arm against her body with his right hand.

2. | Pause . . .

2.5 | B shifts his weight 70% onto his left leg and pushes A's left upper arm with his right hand.
      A neutralizes by shifting her weight back onto her right leg and turning her torso counter-clockwise to her left.

114. Separate Right, Ward Off Left, and Chop with Fist (right style)

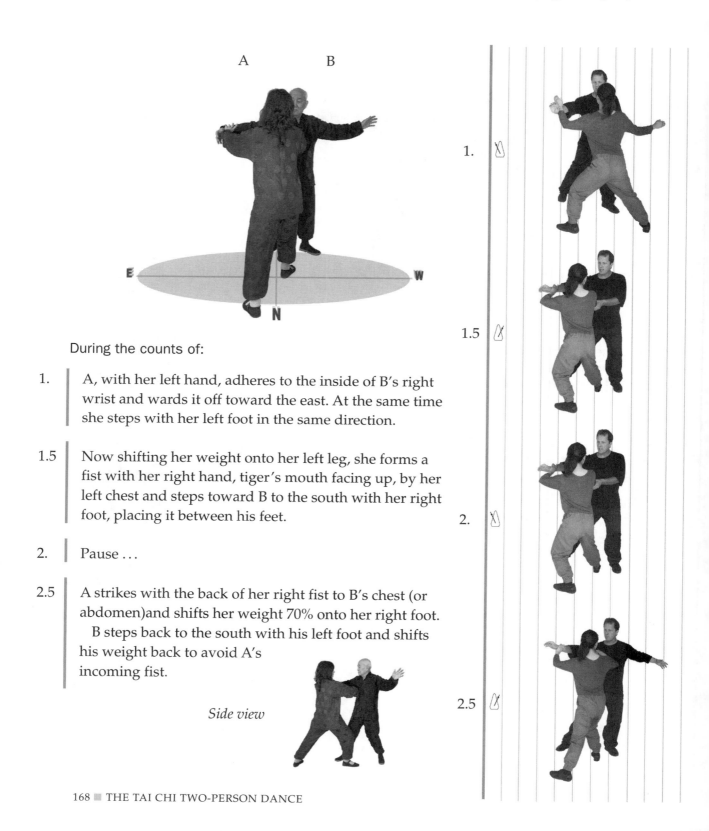

A   B

E

N

W

During the counts of:

1.	A, with her left hand, adheres to the inside of B's right wrist and wards it off toward the east. At the same time she steps with her left foot in the same direction.
1.5	Now shifting her weight onto her left leg, she forms a fist with her right hand, tiger's mouth facing up, by her left chest and steps toward B to the south with her right foot, placing it between his feet.
2.	Pause ...
2.5	A strikes with the back of her right fist to B's chest (or abdomen)and shifts her weight 70% onto her right foot. B steps back to the south with his left foot and shifts his weight back to avoid A's incoming fist.

Side view

1.

1.5

2.

2.5

115. Turn Body Sideways and Punch with Fist (right style)

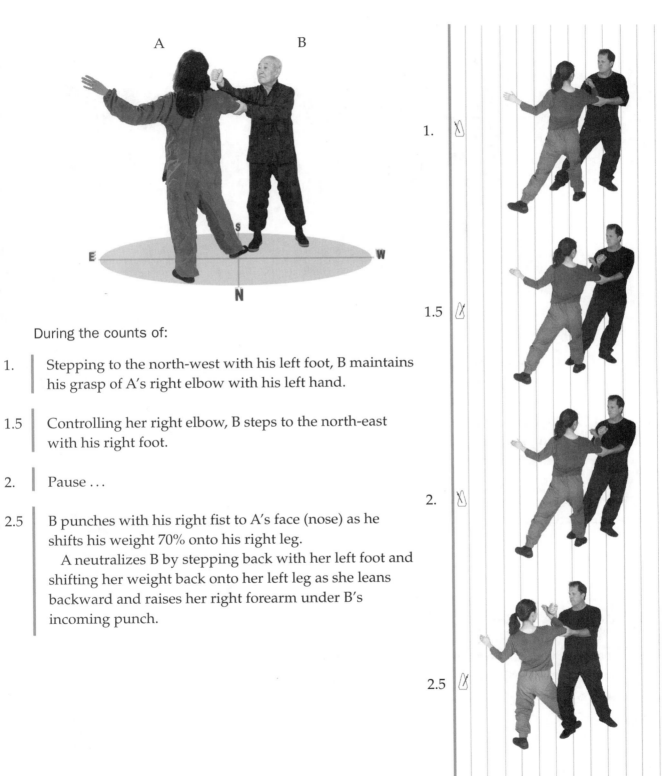

During the counts of:

1. | Stepping to the north-west with his left foot, B maintains his grasp of A's right elbow with his left hand.

1.5 | Controlling her right elbow, B steps to the north-east with his right foot.

2. | Pause ...

2.5 | B punches with his right fist to A's face (nose) as he shifts his weight 70% onto his right leg.
   A neutralizes B by stepping back with her left foot and shifting her weight back onto her left leg as she leans backward and raises her right forearm under B's incoming punch.

116. Step Forward, High Pat on Horse, and Kick with Sole (left style)

A   B

During the counts of:

1.	A, lightly grasping B's right wrist with her right hand, steps with her right foot toward the south.
1.5	Shifting her weight onto her right foot, she uses this momentum to swing her left leg around with her knee and toes raised up to face B to the west. Her left hand circles around past her left ear, palm facing west. While turning she pulls B's right wrist with her right hand to the north, in an attempt to throw him off balance.
2.	Pause . . .
2.5	A kicks with her left sole to B's right knee and strikes with her open left palm to B's face. B neutralizes A's striking palm by throwing his head back. At the same time he avoids her kick by shifting his weight onto his left leg and swinging his right leg north to his left.

1.

1.5

2.

2.5

117. White Crane Spreading Wings and Circling Kick and Slap (right style)

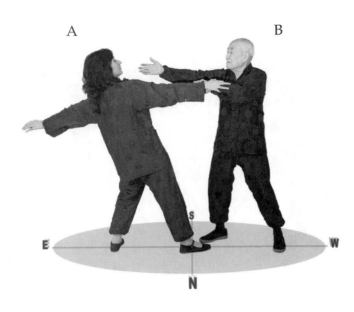

During the counts of:

1. | B, with his weight on his left leg, grasps A's right wrist with his left hand and attaches his right wrist to the inside at A's left wrist.

1.5 | He sweeps A's left leg away to the south with his right leg while pushing A's left wrist toward the south with the back of his right hand.

2. | He then steps with his right foot east toward A . . .

2.5 | . . . and slaps at her face with his open right palm.
A steps back with her left foot and throws her left hand and head back to avoid the slap.

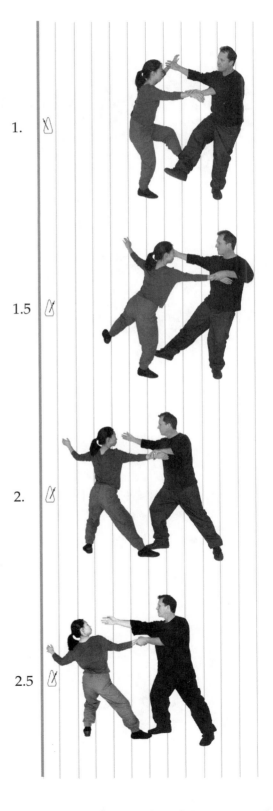

1.

1.5

2.

2.5

118. Turn Body and Lotus Sweep (right style)

A   B

During the counts of:

1. | Circling under B's right wrist with her right hand, . . .

1.5 | . . . A grabs B's right wrist and pulls it north to her right.

2. | A circles her . . .

2.5 | . . . right foot in a clockwise sweeping motion around to strike B's right side (kidney).
    B neutralizes by shifting his weight back and turning his torso, counter-clockwise, away from the kick.

    Both A and B hold their left hands back and open.

1.

1.5

2.

2.5

119. Diagonal Flying Posture (left style)

During the counts of:

1. | B, grasping A's right wrist with his right hand, picks his right foot up and places it back down with his toes facing south.

1.5 | Shifting his weight onto his right foot, he steps behind A with his left foot, toes pointing east, and places his left forearm across A's chest, leaving his left hand open. (see opposite view detail below)

2. | Pause . . .

2.5 | B shifts his weight 70% onto his left leg and, in a "scissors"-like motion of his left arm cutting over his left leg, pushes A by turning his torso counter-clockwise to his left.
    A neutralizes by shifting her weight back onto her left leg.

opposite view

120. Single Whip Squatting Down

A   B

During the counts of:

1. | A grasps B's right wrist with her right hand and, ...

1.5 | ... stepping back to the east with her right leg, pulls B's wrist and arm with her.

2. | Turning her torso to face B ...

2.5 | ... A now strikes with her left-hand fingers to B's groin and then shifts her weight 70% onto her left leg.
    B intercepts A's striking left-hand by adhering to it with his left wrist and moving it slightly south to his right, while at the same time shifting his weight back onto his right leg and turning his torso slightly to his right.

1.

1.5

2.

2.5

121. Diagonal Flying Posture (right style)

During the counts of:

1. | Grasping A's left wrist with his left hand, B turns his left foot to point north and places it in front of A's left foot, forming a "T."

1.5 | He steps behind A with his right foot, toes pointing east, and brings his right arm up across A's chest.

2. | B shifts his weight forward and ...

2.5 | ... strikes in a sweeping motion to his right across A's chest. He has the potential to sweep her left leg with his right leg.

A neutralizes by shifting her weight back onto her right leg. Her right hand extends backward.

122. Strike Tiger (left style)

A   B

During the counts of:

1. | A grasps B's right elbow with her right hand and ...

1.5 | ... withdraws her left hand and foot back to the east. She forms a fist with her left hand, tiger's mouth facing out to the south, by her left hip.

2. | Pause ...

2.5 | She then steps with her left foot to the west on B's right side and punches to his right kidney with her left fist, turning tiger's mouth up as she shifts her weight 70% onto her left leg.

    B neutralizes by shifting his weight back onto his left leg and turning his torso clockwise to his right, away from the incoming punch.

1.

1.5

2.

2.5

123. Turn Body and Chop with Fist (right style)

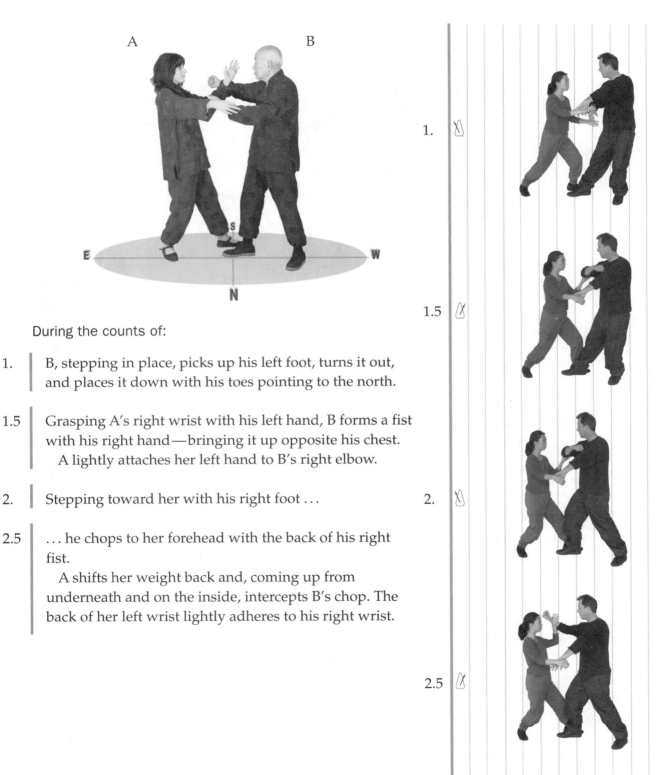

During the counts of:

1. | B, stepping in place, picks up his left foot, turns it out, and places it down with his toes pointing to the north.

1.5 | Grasping A's right wrist with his left hand, B forms a fist with his right hand—bringing it up opposite his chest.
A lightly attaches her left hand to B's right elbow.

2. | Stepping toward her with his right foot ...

2.5 | ... he chops to her forehead with the back of his right fist.
A shifts her weight back and, coming up from underneath and on the inside, intercepts B's chop. The back of her left wrist lightly adheres to his right wrist.

124. Step Back to Chase the Monkey Away (right style)

A   B

1.

1.5

2.

2.5

During the counts of:

1.	A steps back with her left foot and circles her right hand . . .
1.5	. . . around to her right ear as she shifts her weight back onto her left foot.
2.	Pause . . .
2.5	A now strikes to B's face with her open right palm. In order to avoid the strike, B throws his head and left hand back while shifting his weight back onto his left leg.

125. Step Forward and Slap (left style)

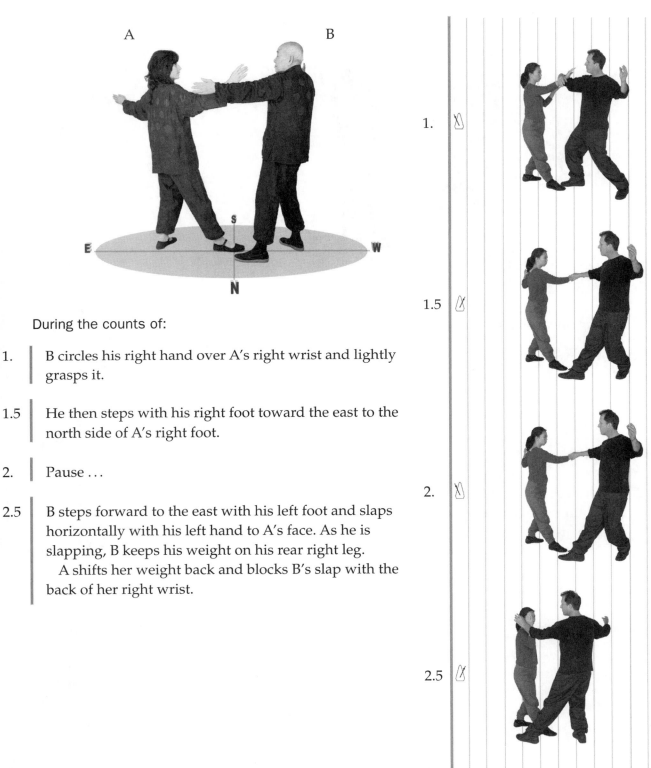

During the counts of:

1. | B circles his right hand over A's right wrist and lightly grasps it.

1.5 | He then steps with his right foot toward the east to the north side of A's right foot.

2. | Pause ...

2.5 | B steps forward to the east with his left foot and slaps horizontally with his left hand to A's face. As he is slapping, B keeps his weight on his rear right leg.
A shifts her weight back and blocks B's slap with the back of her right wrist.

126. Step Back to Chase the Monkey Away (left style)

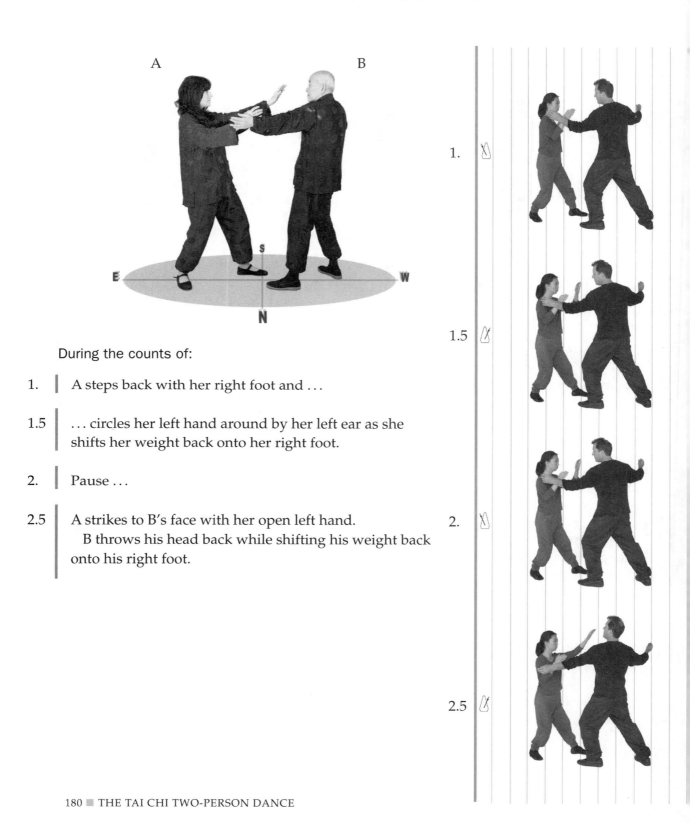

A   B

S
E   W
N

During the counts of:

1. | A steps back with her right foot and ...

1.5 | ... circles her left hand around by her left ear as she shifts her weight back onto her right foot.

2. | Pause ...

2.5 | A strikes to B's face with her open left hand.
B throws his head back while shifting his weight back onto his right foot.

1.

1.5

2.

2.5

127. Step Forward and Slap (right style)

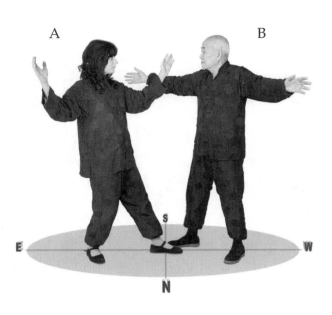

During the counts of:

1.	B circles his left hand over A's left wrist and ...
1.5	... steps with his left foot toward the south-east on her left side.
2.	He then steps with his right foot to the east ...
2.5	... and slaps horizontally with his right hand to A's face. B keeps his weight back on his left leg. A shifts her weight back and blocks B's slap with the back of her left wrist. Both A and B hold their right hands diagonally back and open.

1.

1.5

2.

2.5

128. Step Back to Chase the Monkey Away (right style)

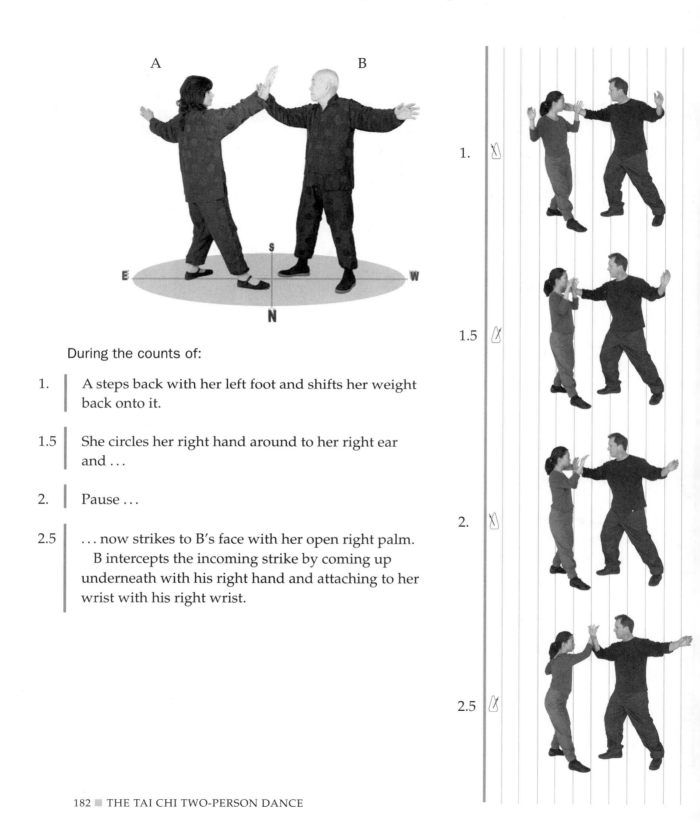

A   B

S

E   W

N

1.

1.5

2.

2.5

During the counts of:

1.	A steps back with her left foot and shifts her weight back onto it.
1.5	She circles her right hand around to her right ear and . . .
2.	Pause . . .
2.5	. . . now strikes to B's face with her open right palm. B intercepts the incoming strike by coming up underneath with his right hand and attaching to her wrist with his right wrist.

129. B: Step Forward to the Seven Stars
A: The Needle at Sea Bottom

A   B

During the counts of:

1.	B brings his left hand up underneath his right hand so that both hands are crossed under A's right wrist (see detail A below).
1.5	He then steps up with his left foot, bringing it even with his right foot. A attaches her left hand to her right wrist.
2.	B then kicks with the top of his right foot ...
2.5	... to A's groin. A grabs B's right wrist with her right hand and, attaching her left hand to her right wrist for support (see detail B below), pulls him downward as she stepsback with her right leg and shifts her weight back onto it.

A   B

1.

1.5

2.

2.5

130. Fan Through the Back

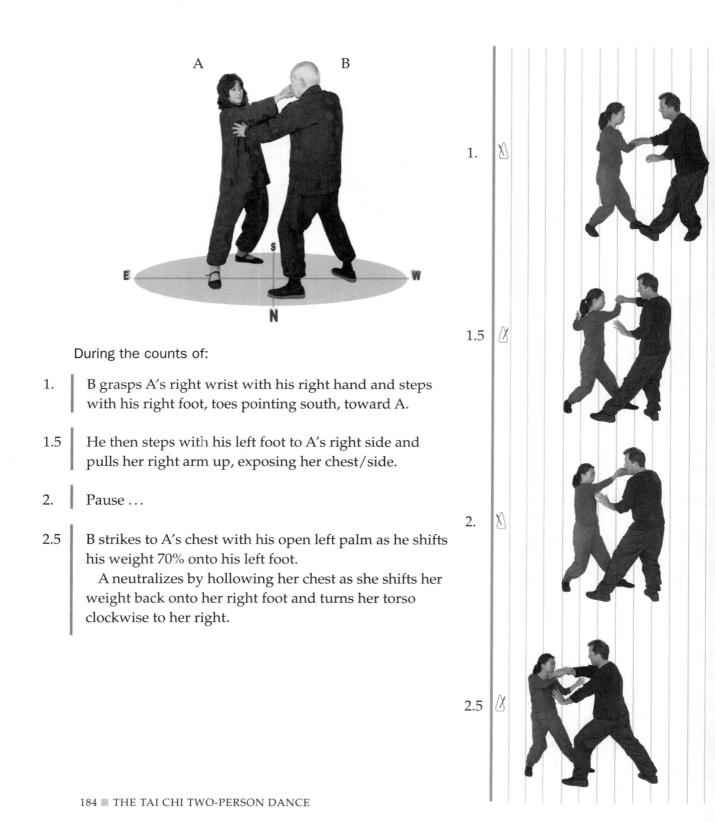

During the counts of:

1. | B grasps A's right wrist with his right hand and steps with his right foot, toes pointing south, toward A.

1.5 | He then steps with his left foot to A's right side and pulls her right arm up, exposing her chest/side.

2. | Pause ...

2.5 | B strikes to A's chest with his open left palm as he shifts his weight 70% onto his left foot.
  A neutralizes by hollowing her chest as she shifts her weight back onto her right foot and turns her torso clockwise to her right.

131. Play Guitar

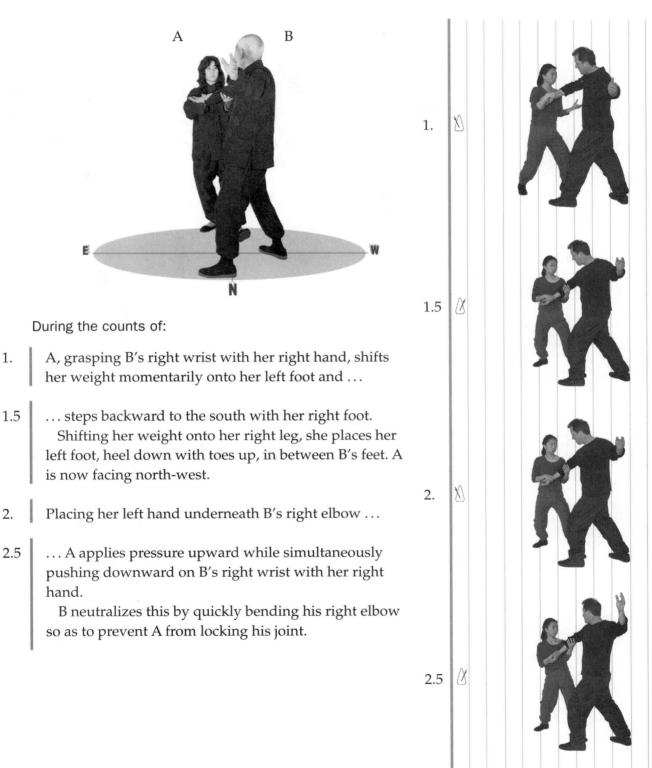

During the counts of:

1.   A, grasping B's right wrist with her right hand, shifts her weight momentarily onto her left foot and ...

1.5   ... steps backward to the south with her right foot.
    Shifting her weight onto her right leg, she places her left foot, heel down with toes up, in between B's feet. A is now facing north-west.

2.   Placing her left hand underneath B's right elbow ...

2.5   ... A applies pressure upward while simultaneously pushing downward on B's right wrist with her right hand.
    B neutralizes this by quickly bending his right elbow so as to prevent A from locking his joint.

132. Bend the Bow and Shoot the Tiger

B A

1.

1.5

2.

2.5

During the counts of:

1. | B grasps A's right wrist with his right hand and steps with his right foot to the east.

1.5 | Shifting his weight onto his right foot, he pivots on it and swings his left foot clockwise around to the southeast so that his toes end up facing south-west. With this swinging motion of his torso B pulls A's right wrist to the north, exposing her right side.

2. | With his left hand, B forms a fist, tiger's mouth up . . .

2.5 | . . . and punches with the bottom side of his fist to A's right side/kidney.
     A neutralizes by hollowing her chest, turning her waist clockwise, and shifting her weight back onto her left leg.

133. Turn Body and Single Whip (right style)

During the counts of:

1.	A, shifting her weight slightly onto her right foot, takes a small step to the north with her left foot.
1.5	At the same time she lightly grasps B's right wrist with her left hand. She then steps east toward B with her right foot and ...
2.	Pause ...
2.5	... turning her torso to face him, she strikes to his chest with the back of her right hand "whip," fingers pointing downward (see detail below). B hollows his chest and shifts his weight back onto his left leg.

134. Punch Under the Elbow

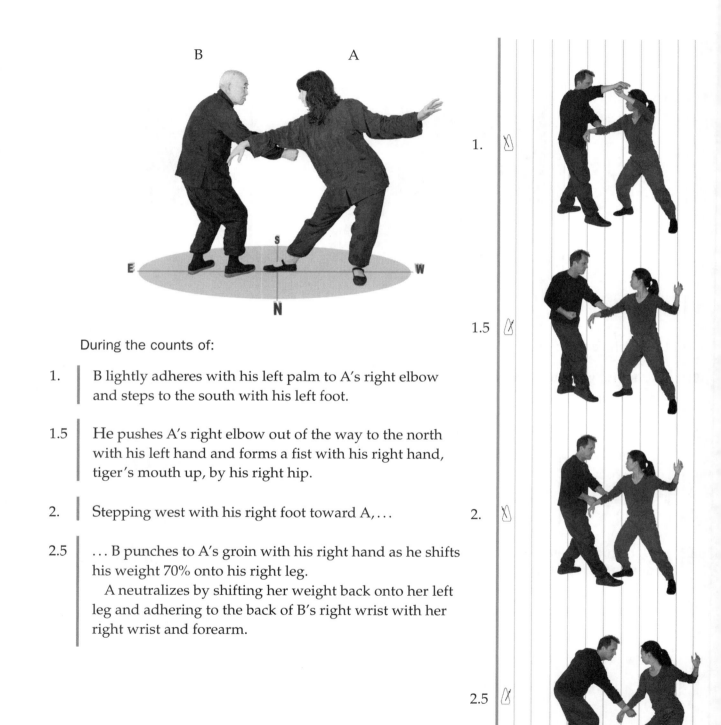

B   A

During the counts of:

1. | B lightly adheres with his left palm to A's right elbow and steps to the south with his left foot.

1.5 | He pushes A's right elbow out of the way to the north with his left hand and forms a fist with his right hand, tiger's mouth up, by his right hip.

2. | Stepping west with his right foot toward A, . . .

2.5 | . . . B punches to A's groin with his right hand as he shifts his weight 70% onto his right leg.
    A neutralizes by shifting her weight back onto her left leg and adhering to the back of B's right wrist with her right wrist and forearm.

1.

1.5

2.

2.5

135. Join Hands

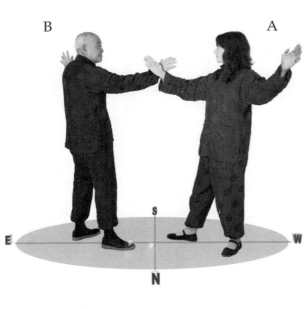

B   A

During the counts of:

1.	A and B adjust the position of their feet to each other and ...
1.5	... join their right hands together at the wrists ...
2.	... and rise up into ...
2.5	... the "Join Hands" posture. Both have their right foot forward, weight back on their left foot, and are joined at the back of their right wrists.

1.

1.5

2.

2.5

Section 9

Postures 136–147

136. A: Turn Body, Pull, and Split
B: Step Forward Right, Left, Right, Elbow and Shoulder Stroke

A   B

E ———————————— W

N

1.

1.5

2.

2.5

During the counts of:

1. | A, pivoting on her left foot, turns it to point south and grasps B's right wrist with her right hand and pulls B to the west.
    B allows himself to be pulled, stepping with his right foot to the south-west.

1.5 | Shifting her weight onto her left foot, A pulls B with her as she swings her torso and right foot around to face west. A attaches her left elbow to B's right elbow.
    B catches up with A's pulling motion by stepping to the west with his left foot.

2. | A continues to pull B around using the "roll back" posture.
    B gets around A's splitting action by stepping again with his right foot to the north and ...

2.5 | ... strikes to A's left side with his right shoulder.
    A shifts her weight back onto her right leg.

137. A: Slap
B: Ward Off

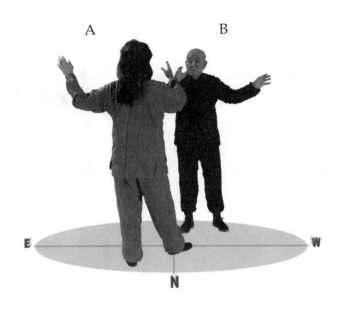

A   B

E   N   W

During the counts of:

1. | A, keeping her left forearm attached to B's elbow,...

1.5 | ... circles her right hand around and ...

2. | ... slaps at B's face with her open palm while ...

2.5 | ... stepping forward toward B with her right foot.
B brings his right hand up to ward off the incoming strike and steps back to the south with his left foot.

A and B both come into the "Join Hands" position (A facing south, B facing north).

1.

1.5

2.

2.5

138. B: Turn Body, Pull, and Split
A: Step Forward Right, Left, Right, Elbow and Shoulder Stroke

1.

1.5

2.

2.5

During the counts of:

1.	B, pivoting on his left foot, turns it to point south-east and grasps A's right wrist with his right hand and pulls A to the south.
1.5	Shifting his weight onto his left foot, B pulls A with him as he swings his torso and right foot around to face south-east. B attaches his left elbow to A's right elbow. A allows herself to be pulled, stepping with her right foot to the south.
2.	B continues to pull A around, "splitting" her right arm. A catches up with B's pulling motion by stepping south-west with her left foot.
2.5	A gets around B's splitting action by stepping again with her right foot to the west and striking to B's left side with her right shoulder. B shifts his weight back onto his right leg.

139. B: Slap
A: Ward Off

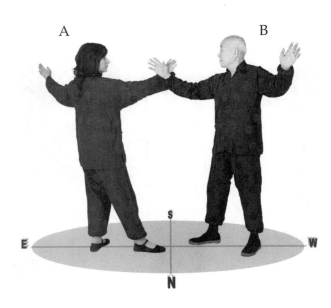

During the counts of:

1.	B, keeping his left forearm attached to A's elbow, circles ...
1.5	... his right hand around toward his right ear. A steps back to the east with her left foot.
2.	B slaps at A's face with his open right palm while at the same time stepping forward toward A with his right foot.
2.5	A brings her right hand up to ward off the incoming strike. A and B both come into the "Join Hands" position. A faces west, B faces east.

140. Step Forward and Choke the Throat (left style)

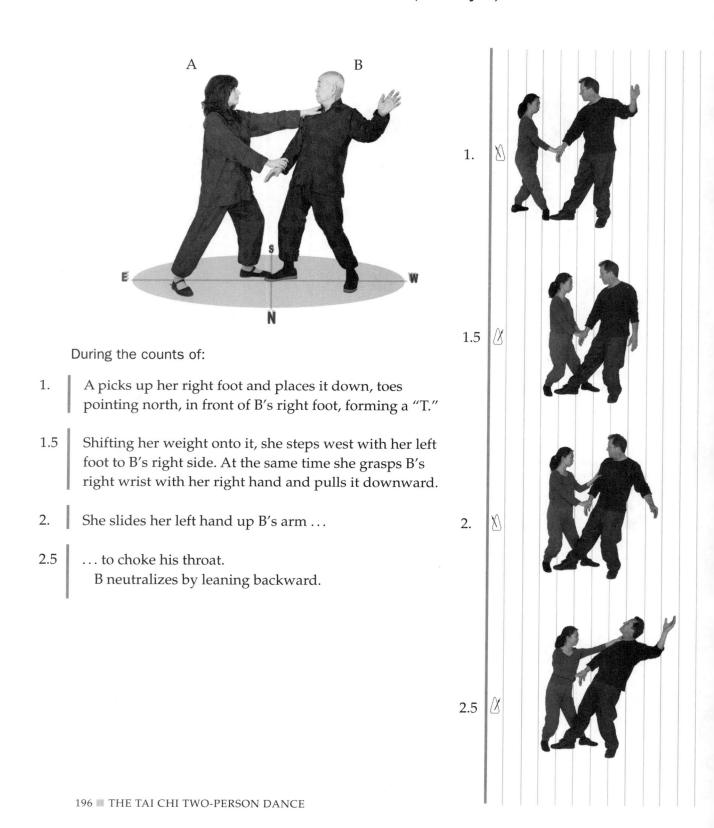

A   B

During the counts of:

1.	A picks up her right foot and places it down, toes pointing north, in front of B's right foot, forming a "T."
1.5	Shifting her weight onto it, she steps west with her left foot to B's right side. At the same time she grasps B's right wrist with her right hand and pulls it downward.
2.	She slides her left hand up B's arm ...
2.5	... to choke his throat. B neutralizes by leaning backward.

1.

1.5

2.

2.5

141. Embrace the Tiger and Return to the Mountain

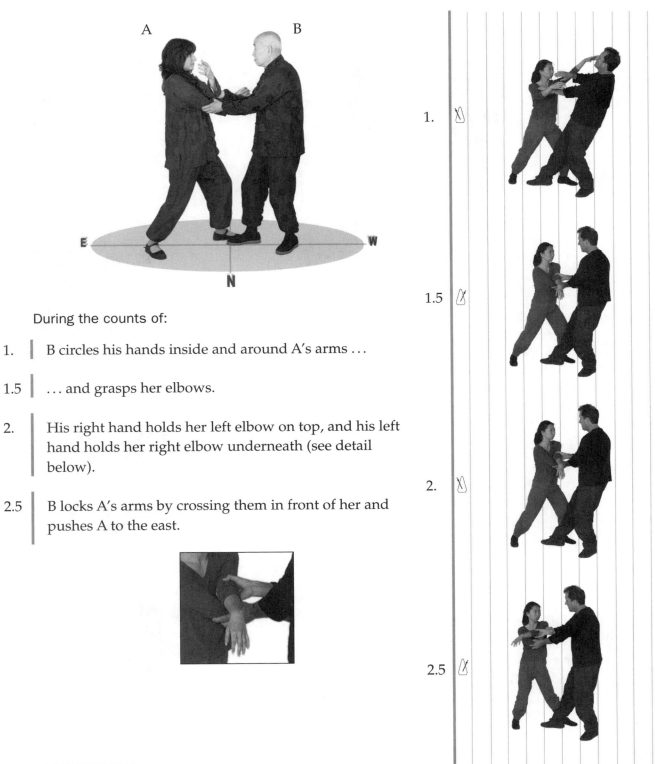

During the counts of:

1. | B circles his hands inside and around A's arms . . .

1.5 | . . . and grasps her elbows.

2. | His right hand holds her left elbow on top, and his left hand holds her right elbow underneath (see detail below).

2.5 | B locks A's arms by crossing them in front of her and pushes A to the east.

142. A: Turn Body, Roll Back, and Lift Hands
B: Step Forward, Turn Body, and Lift Hands

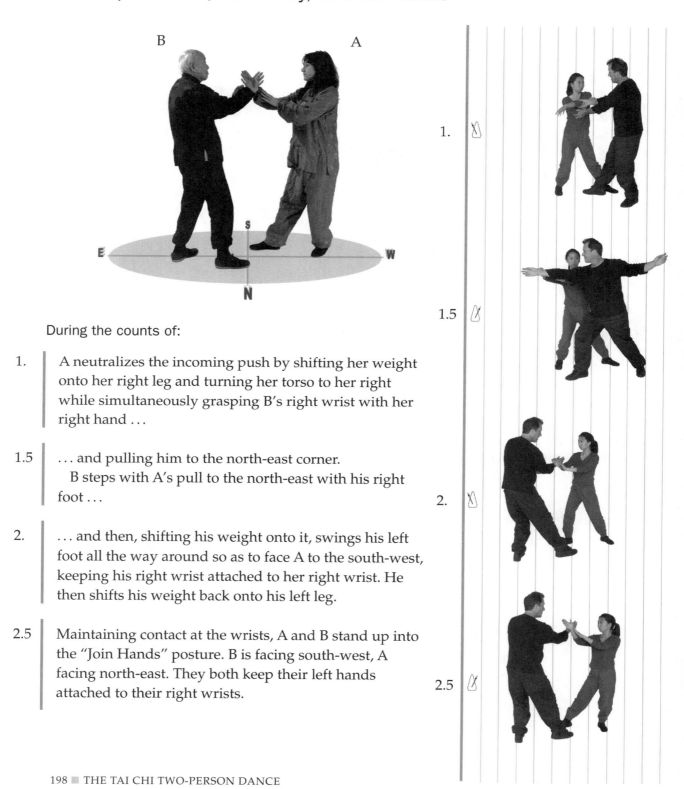

During the counts of:

1. | A neutralizes the incoming push by shifting her weight onto her right leg and turning her torso to her right while simultaneously grasping B's right wrist with her right hand ...

1.5 | ... and pulling him to the north-east corner.
    B steps with A's pull to the north-east with his right foot ...

2. | ... and then, shifting his weight onto it, swings his left foot all the way around so as to face A to the south-west, keeping his right wrist attached to her right wrist. He then shifts his weight back onto his left leg.

2.5 | Maintaining contact at the wrists, A and B stand up into the "Join Hands" posture. B is facing south-west, A facing north-east. They both keep their left hands attached to their right wrists.

143. A: Step Back to Ride the Tiger

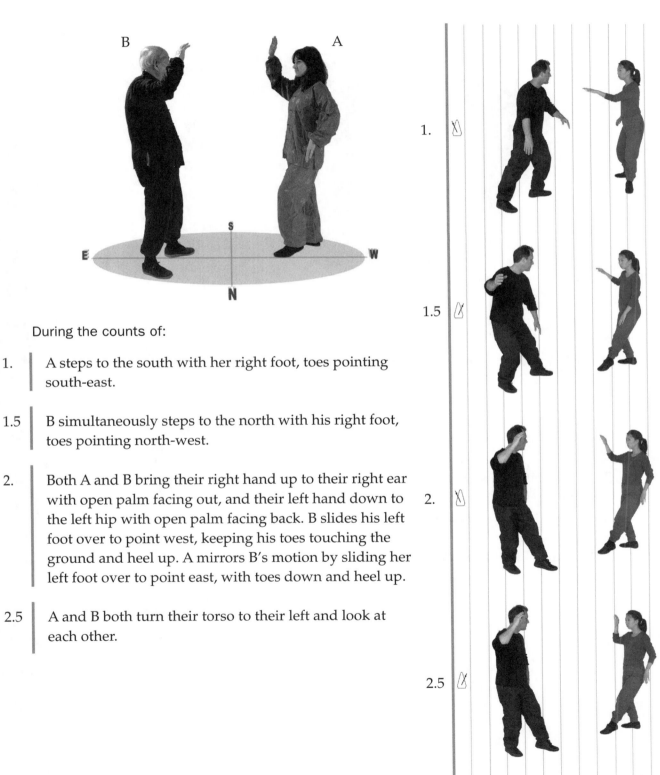

During the counts of:

1. | A steps to the south with her right foot, toes pointing south-east.

1.5 | B simultaneously steps to the north with his right foot, toes pointing north-west.

2. | Both A and B bring their right hand up to their right ear with open palm facing out, and their left hand down to the left hip with open palm facing back. B slides his left foot over to point west, keeping his toes touching the ground and heel up. A mirrors B's motion by sliding her left foot over to point east, with toes down and heel up.

2.5 | A and B both turn their torso to their left and look at each other.

144. A: Crossing Hands

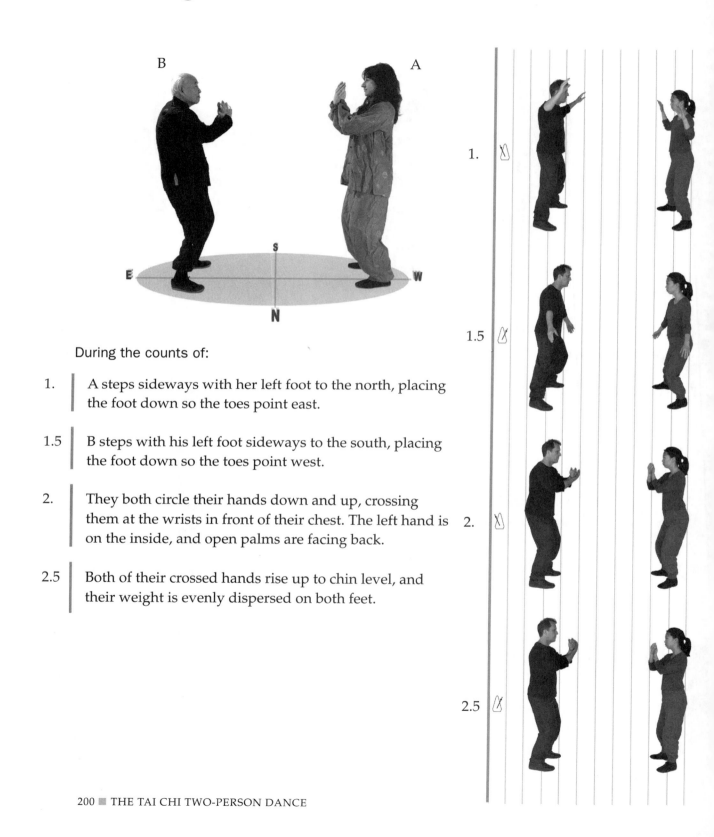

B   A

During the counts of:

1.	A steps sideways with her left foot to the north, placing the foot down so the toes point east.
1.5	B steps with his left foot sideways to the south, placing the foot down so the toes point west.
2.	They both circle their hands down and up, crossing them at the wrists in front of their chest. The left hand is on the inside, and open palms are facing back.
2.5	Both of their crossed hands rise up to chin level, and their weight is evenly dispersed on both feet.

1.

1.5

2.

2.5

145. Conclusion of Tai Chi Dance

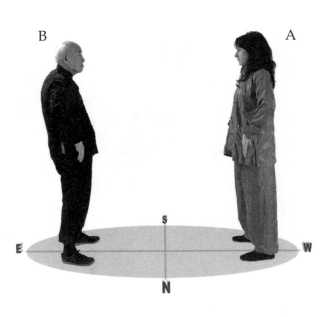

During the counts of:

1. | A and B together bring their hands ...

1.5 | ... down to their ...

2. | ... sides as they straighten out their legs.

2.5 | With open palms facing back, they both raise their hands up to hip-pocket level.

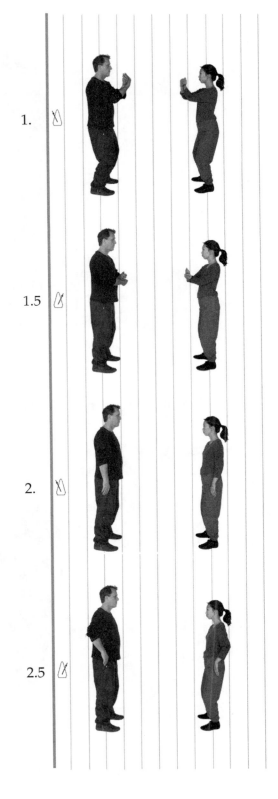

146. Closing Bow to Your Partner

A and B bow to each other to the count of two beats and then turn to face north and bow again to the count of two beats.

147. Closing Bow Forward

9

Conclusion

A question that teachers often hear is: "How long will it take me to learn Tai Chi?" T.T. Liang probably answered this best when referring to himself:

> *... The more I learn, the less I feel I know.*
> *The theory and philosophy of Tai Chi is so profound and abstruse!*
> *I must continue to study forever and forever...*
> *It is the only way to improve and better myself.*

When first studying Tai Chi with T.T. Liang I was quite curious about tenacious or intrinsic energy, so I asked him to show me how I could develop it. I was quite pleased when he told me that he would show me an exercise that if practiced regularly would yield great results. He brought me to the middle of our studio, where there was a pillar. Facing it with one foot back in a "bow and arrow stance," I was instructed to place both my hands at about chest height on the pillar. Then he said to completely relax and make the smallest and gentlest push against it with my whole body moving in one motion from foot to hand. That was it. Just repeat that motion over and over. This was easy, I thought, so I asked him, "How long will this take for me to 'get it'?" As he walked back to his room he muttered, "Oh ... fifteen years at least."

Learning Tai Chi is like peeling an onion: when you comprehend one layer it reveals another that you were not aware of. It is an art full of subtleties and gradations of subtleties. The skills discussed in this book are there to aid in your studies. They are like a scaffolding set up to help build a structure. When the structure is built, the scaffolding should be shed.

I would often stop at the studio after classes were over to talk with Liang and practice Pushing Hands with him. One night he was expecting a visitor, so while waiting for him to arrive we "pushed" for a while.

As we maneuvered back and forth I managed to get him into a defect position where he was off balance on his back leg. Just as I was about to push him he shouted, "Stop!"

"Why?" I asked, quite sure that I could have pushed him.

"You can't do what you're about to do because you're double-weighted," he said. He went on to explain that "your weight is on your right foot and you're trying to push with your right hand. This is called 'being double-weighted' and puts you into an out-of-balance and awkward position."

So I backed off thinking, "OK—whatever you say…."

Eventually Liang's visitor arrived and they sat and talked for a while. Liang then called me over and said, "He wants to push hands with you."

It is the custom not to push with the teacher but with the senior student instead, so I agreed. We started maneuvering each other back and forth, and I managed to get him into exactly the same position as I had previously put Liang. As he teetered off balance I remembered the advice Liang had just given me, so I stopped.

Liang looked at me in wonderment and said, "What are you waiting for? Why don't you push him?"

"I can't," I explained. "You told me that if I push from this position I will be double-weighted and off balance."

Liang laughed and said, "So what, if it works, use it!"

Appendix A

Tai Chi Two-Person Dance Posture List

(Note: T.T. Liang's original Dance consisted of 175 postures. The set presented here is exactly the same order of his 175 postures, but I have given some postures the same number, as they are performed during the same count, resulting in 147 postures.)

1. A & B: Opening Bow (N/N)
2. A & B: Opening Bow to Your Partner (E/W)
3. A & B: Preparation (E/W)

Section One

4. B: Step Forward and Chop (W)
5. A: Roll Back—right style (NE)
6. B: Shoulder Stroke—right style (W)
7. A: Slap—right style (E)
8. B: Roll Back—right style (NW)
9. A: Shoulder Stroke—right style (SE)
10. B: Push (SW)
11. A: Roll Back—left style (N)
12. B: Shoulder Stroke—left style (SE)
13. A: Slap—left style (NW)
14. B: Roll Back—left style (NE)
15. A: Shoulder Stroke—left style (SW)
16. B: Push (E)
    A: Withdraw Body and Roll Back (W)
17. A & B: Join Hands (W/E)

Section Two

18. A: Step Forward and Punch (W)
19. B: Deflect and Chop (E)

20. A: Step Forward and Shoulder Stroke (W)
21. B: Withdraw Step and Strike Tiger (W)
22. A: Elbow Stroke (E)
23. B: Push with Right Hand (W)
24. A: Chop with Fist (E)
25. B: Shoulder Stroke—right style (W)
26. A: Withdraw, Step, and Strike Tiger—left style (SE)
27. B: Chop with Fist and A & B Join Hands (NW/SE)

Section Three

28. A: Block and Punch Upward (NE)
29. B: Turn Body and Push (SW)
30. A: Fold and Chop with Fist (NE)
31. B: Deflect and Punch (SW)
32. A: Horizontal Split (N)
33. B: Change Step and Parting Wild Horse's Mane—left style (SW)
34. A: Strike Tiger—right style (NE)
35. B: Turn Body, Withdraw, Step, and Roll Back (NE)
36. A & B: Join Hands (SW/NE)

Section Four: Ta Lu

37. A: Pull (SW)
    B: Ward Off (NE)
38. A: Split (SW)
    B: Roll Back (NE)
39. A: Elbow Stroke (SW)
40. B: Push (NE)
41. A: Shoulder Stroke (SW)
42. B: Press (NE)
43. A & B: Join Hands (NW/SE)
44. B: Pull (SE)
    A: Ward Off (NW)
45. B: Split (SE) / A: Roll Back (NW)
46. B: Elbow Stroke (SE)
47. A: Push (NW)
48. B: Shoulder Stroke (SE)
49. A: Press (NW)
50. A & B: Join Hands (E/W)

Section Five

51. A: Step Forward and Shoulder
    Stroke—left style (NW)
52. B: Turn Body and Push (S)
53. A: Separate Hands and Kick with Sole
    (N)
54. B: Punch to the Groin (S)
55. A: Step Forward, Pull, and Split (N)
56. B: Change Step and Fair Lady
    Weaving with a Shuttle Right (S)
57. A: Left Ward Off and Right Chop with
    Fist (N)
58. B: White Crane Spreading Wings and
    Kick with Left Sole (S)
59. A: Step Forward and Shoulder
    Stroke—left style (NW)
60. B: Step Back and Hammer A's Left
    Arm (N)
61. A: Turn Body and Roll Back (S)
62. B: Strike with Two Fists (N)

63. A: Step Forward and Push with Two
    Hands (S)
64. B: Squatting Down, Ward Off, and
    Punch (N)
65. A: Push with Left Hand (SW)
66. B: Twist A's Right Arm (E)
67. A: Take Advantage and Push (W)
68. B: Neutralize and Strike with Right
    Palm (E)
69. A: Neutralize and Push (W)
70. B: Neutralize and Elbow Stroke (E)
71. A & B: Join Hands (W/E)

Section Six: "Pushing Hands" Practice

(Fixed step)

72. B: Step Forward with Left Foot and
    Push (E)
    A: Step Back with Right Foot, Ward
    Off, and Roll Back (W)
73. B: Press (E)
    A: Neutralize (W)
74. A: Push (W)
    B: Ward Off and Roll Back (E)
75. A: Press (W)
    B: Neutralize (W)
76. B: Push (E)
    A: Ward Off and Roll Back (W)
77. B: Press (E)
    A: Neutralize (W)
78. A & B: Circle Hands (W/E)
79. A: Step Forward with Right Foot and
    Push (W)
    B: Step Back with Left Foot, Ward Off,
    and Roll Back (E)
80. A: Press (W)
    B: Neutralize (W)
81. B: Push (W)
    A: Ward Off and Roll Back (E)
82. B: Press (W)
    A: Neutralize (W)

82. A: Push (E)
    B: Ward Off and Roll Back (W)
84. A: Press (E)
    B: Neutralize (W)
85. B: Push (E)
    A: Ward Off and Roll Back (W)
86. B: Press (E)
    A: Neutralize
(Active Step and Circling)
87. A: Hands Circling Counter-clockwise
    and Step Forward with Left Foot (W)
    B: Hands Circling Clockwise and Step
    Back with Right Foot (E)
88. A: Hands Circling Counter-clockwise
    and Step Forward with Right Foot (W)
    B: Hands Circling Clockwise and Step
    Back with Left Foot (E)
89. A: Hands Circling Counter-clockwise
    and Step Forward with Left Foot (W)
    B: Hands Circling Clockwise and Step
    Back with Right Foot (E)
90. A: Hands Circling Clockwise and Step
    Forward with Right Foot (W)
    B: Hands Circling Counter-clockwise
    and Step Back with Left Foot (E)
91. A: Hands Circling Clockwise and Step
    Forward with Left Foot (W)
    B: Hands Circling Counter-clockwise
    and Step Back with Right Foot (E)
92. A: Hands Circling Clockwise and Step
    Forward with Right Foot (W)
    B: Hands Circling Counter-clockwise
    and Step Back with Left Foot (E)

Section Seven

93. A: Step Forward and Horizontal Split—
    right style (W)
94. B: Change Step and Hammer A's Right
    Arm (SE)
95. A: Strike Tiger—right style (NW)

96. B: Turn Body, Withdraw Step, and Roll
    Back (SW)
97. A: Step Forward and Shoulder Stroke—
    left style (E)
98. B: Press (S)
99. A: Change Step, Separate Both Hands,
    and Shoulder Stroke (N)
100. B: Change Step, Turn Body, and
     Shoulder Stroke—left style (E)
101. A: Striking Elbow—right style (W)
102. B: Turn Body and Golden Rooster
     Stands on One Leg—left style (E)
     A: Step Back and Neutralize (W)
103. B: Separate Both Hands, Step Forward,
     and Kick with Sole (E)
     A: Step Back and Neutralize (W)
104. A: Turn Body, Step Forward, and
     Shoulder Stroke—left style (W)
105. B: Step Back and Hammer B's Arm
106. A: Turn Body, Change Step, and
     Separate Foot—right style (W)
     B: Separate Both Hands and Brush
     Knee—right style (E)
107. A: Turn Body, Change Step, and
     Separate Foot—left style (W)
     B: Separate Both Hands and Brush
     Knee—left style (E)
108. A: Change Hands and Shoulder
     Stroke—right style (W)
109. B: Return Shoulder Stroke (E)

Section Eight

110. A: Step Forward and Grasp the
     Sparrow's Tail—left style (W)
111. B: Waving Hands in the Clouds—right
     style (SW)
112. A: Step Forward and Grasp the
     Sparrow's Tail—right style (W)
113. B: Waving Hands in Clouds—left style
114. A: Separate Right, Ward Off Left, and

Chop with Fist—right style (S)

115. B: Turn Body Sideways and Punch
with Fist—right style (NE)

116. A: Step Forward, High Pat on Horse,
and Kick with Sole—left style (W)

117. B: White Crane Spreading Wings and
Circling Kick and Slap—right style
(E)

118. A: Turn Body and Lotus Sweep—
right style (W

119. B: Diagonal Flying Posture—left style
(E)

120. A: Single Whip Squatting Down (W)

121. B: Diagonal Flying Posture—right
style (E)

122. A: Strike Tiger—left style (SW)

123. B: Turn Body and Chop with Fist—
right style (E)

124. A: Step Back to Chase the Monkey
Away—right style (W)

125. B: Step Forward and Slap—left style
(E)

126. A: Step Back to Chase the Monkey
Away—left style (W)

127. B: Step Forward and Slap—right style
(E)

128. A: Step Back to Chase the Monkey
Away—right style (W)

129. B: Step Forward to the Seven Stars (E)
A: The Needle at Sea Bottom (W)

130. B: Fan Through the Back (E)

131. A: Play Guitar (N)

132. B: Bend the Bow and Shoot the Tiger
(SW)

133. A: Turn Body and Single Whip—right
style (E)

134. B: Punch Under the Elbow (W)

135. A & B: Join Hands (E & W)

Section Nine

136. A: Turn Body, Pull, and Split (W)
B: Step Forward: Right, Left, Right,
Elbow and Shoulder Stroke (N)

137. A: Slap (S)
B: Ward Off (N)

138. B: Turn Body, Pull, and Split (W)
A: Step Forward: Right, Left, Right,
Elbow and Shoulder Stroke (N)

139. B: Slap (E)
A: Ward Off (W)

140. A: Step Forward and Choke the
Throat—left style (W)

141. B: Embrace the Tiger and Return to
the Mountain (E)

142. A: Turn Body, Roll Back, and Lift
Hands (NE)
B: Step Forward, Turn Body, and Lift
Hands (W)

143. A & B: Step Back to Ride the Tiger
(E/W)

144. A & B: Crossing Hands (E/W)

145. A & B: Conclusion of Tai Chi Dance
(E/W)

146. A & B: Closing Bow to Your Partner
(E/W)

147. A & B: Closing Bow Forward (N/N)

Appendix B

Glossary of Terms

Bow Stance: This stance resembles a "bow and arrow." Your forward leg forms the bow with 70% of your weight on it and your rear leg is the arrow. Your forward knee does not pass beyond the toes and your rear leg remains slightly bent with the foot turned out at a 45-degree angle (see: Shoulder-Width Stance).

Catch Step: A step with a leg that is already weighted. This is done by briefly shifting your weight into the unweighted leg (1) and then stepping (2).

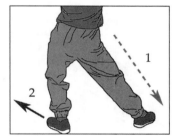

Central Equilibrium: A state of maintaining your balance. When you don't lean in any direction and hold no residual tension in your body this allows your weight to sink downward. A cone with the majority of its weight on the ground is a good example of "central equilibrium."

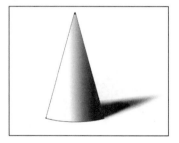

Feint: A pretend rigidity or aggressive action performed in order to entice your opponent to take action against you. This gives you the opportunity to neutralize his incoming force and detect his line of balance.

Floating: When your center of gravity rises upwards. Caused by tensing and constricting your body.

Grasp: Different from "grab"—to lightly hold with the potential for action.

Horse Stance: A stance that mimics riding a horse. With the body squatting down, both of your feet are wide apart with the toes facing forward. In this position your weight is never distributed evenly on both legs while engaged with your partner and in motion.

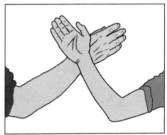

Join Hands: A beginning and ending posture where both partners lightly join their right (or left) hands at the back of their wrists. From this position they "listen" to each other's slightest movements and intentions and initiate any sequence of movements, either choreographed or free-form.

Lock: To fully extend and hold any of your opponent's joints: wrists, elbows, knees, shoulders, etc.

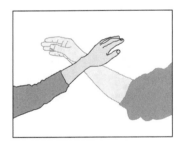

Open Hand Hold: To adhere, guide, and control your partner with your open hand.

Press: By pressing your forearm against your partner you can control their movements and issue force. You follow and respond with the full length of your forearm: from the wrist to the elbow. Your opposite hand is attached to your wrist for support.

Neutralize: To counteract the effect of an incoming force. Using any part of your body you meet your partner's incoming movement, adhere to it without resistance, and guide it to one side—deflecting its potential effect away from yourself.

Root: The ability to allow your weight to pass through your relaxed body into the floor. Your feet, in particular, stay completely relaxed without any tensing of the toes.

Separate: When both hands of your partner are on your body you adhere to the inside of them with both of your hands and split them outward. This can cause your opponent to lose his balance and opens up the possibility of attaching to his chest and issuing.

Shoulder Stroke: Stepping forward and striking your partner with your shoulder, side, or hip. The striking side arm remains close to your body and the hand protects your groin. The opposite hand remains close by or attached to the striking side arm for back-up support.

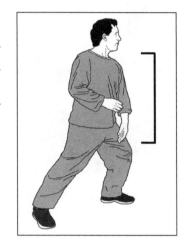

Shoulder-Width Stance: The most stable stance and the basic foot position for many postures in Tai Chi. Your forward foot is placed with its heel on the outer edge of a square. The heel of your other foot is placed on the opposite diagonal corner with its toes turned out at a 45 degree angle. The width of the square is approximately that of your shoulders.

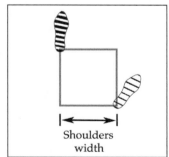

Single Whip: The "whip" is formed by your hand bent down at the wrist, with the fingers and thumb all touching each other as though "picking up a drop of water." The top of your hand strikes toward your partner with the potential of unfolding into a "snake palm" (see: Snake Palm).

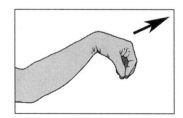

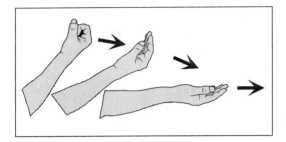

Snake Palm: Your fingers straighten (strike out) from your folded hand or fist.

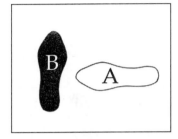

"T" Position: When stepping around your partner you will occasionally adjust and place your foot (B) in a "T" position in front of your partner's forward foot (A).

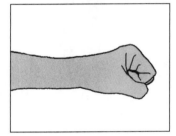

Tiger's Mouth: When forming a fist, the empty space created by the thumb and index finger is called the "tiger's mouth."

Jonathan Russell, "eldest" and senior student of Master T.T. Liang, has studied and taught Tai Chi for more than thirty years. He began his Tai Chi studies with Master Liang in the late sixties. Together they co-founded The Tai Chi Dance Association, setting up numerous schools in the Boston area. Russell worked closely with Liang on producing his now-classic book *Tai Chi for Health and Self-Defense.* Over the fifteen years they worked together they documented in photographs and film all of Master Liang's complete set of Tai Chi exercises. Russell has since traveled extensively throughout the United States giving demonstrations and lectures. He currently lives in San Francisco, where he teaches, writes books, and produces videos on Tai Chi. The readers of the newspaper *The San Francisco Weekly* recently voted his Tai Chi class "Best Of" San Francisco. He can be contacted at: www.TaiChiSF.com.